THE HARD CORPS

COMBAT TRAINING FOR THE MAN OF GOD

DAI HANKEY

The Hard Corps
© Dai Hankey 2012. Reprinted 2019.

Published by:
The Good Book Company

thegoodbook.com | www.thegoodbook.co.uk
thegoodbook.com.au | thegoodbook.co.nz | thegoodbook.co.in

ISBN: 9781905564347 | Printed in India

Design by André Parker

CONTENTS

This book is dedicated to the following:

My dad
For teaching me to embrace adventure, face my fears and be strong in the Lord.

My brothers in Christ
Every man who has ever stood with me, battled alongside me, prayed for me, encouraged me, challenged me, inspired me and pointed me to Jesus. You know who you are!

My sons, Josiah and Ezra:
I love you so much. I pray that the King of all kings will capture your hearts and raise you up as mighty gospel warriors who will do great exploits in His name and for His glory.

INTRO

So the other day I was chillin' on my sofa when my three-year-old son, Josiah, came and stood in front of me demanding my attention. He was sporting a bizarre multi-coloured contraption on his head that he had meticulously hand-crafted out of Popoids[1]. I think it was a crown. Or maybe a helmet. In his hand was a smaller Popoid creation that he informed me was a radio—though it later took on a new identity as an octopus.

"Daddy, I'm a soldier of Jesus!" he enthusiastically announced.

Oh boy!

Truth is, as nuts as he looked, deep down I was buzzin' that in my little boy's whacky world of crazy play he was, in his own unique way, wanting to line up in the ranks of the army of the King of kings.

That's my greatest desire for him, as it is for all my kids.

However, one day Joey is going to wake up and realise that if he's going to fight for King Jesus, he'll need to be armed

---

1 Popoids is a colourful plastic construction kit for kids that consists of weird shapes that can be connected by pipes that bend, twist and click together.

with more than quirky, home-made plastic weapons... even if they do have the ability to miraculously transform into octopuses!

He's going to grow up in a world at war with God. A world that is hell-bent on distracting him from the cause of Jesus, the power of the gospel and the hope of glory.

The reality is that the relentless pressures that my sons are going to face as they grow up are the same ones that are assailing you and me right now—the pressure to conform, to be accepted, to prove yourself, to please yourself, to do whatever it takes to earn love and respect.

The solution, however, isn't to bubble wrap them and hide them away from the horrors of war. Rather, it's to train them to fight and to prevail. To model what it is to be a true man of God. A soldier of Jesus.

So what does that kind of man look like?

Well, the good news is that, contrary to popular belief, there's not a single verse in the Bible to suggest that when a man starts to follow Christ he has to hand in his testicles at the door. Far from it. Scripture teaches that men should be strong, adventurous and willing to fight for what matters! As such we should seek to emulate the heroes of the Bible, who were passionate, courageous, uncompromising, and spiritually solid.

Who are these heroes?

Obviously the greatest example is Jesus Himself—the über hero. It's impossible not to be impressed by Him, both as the cross-carrying King of mercy, and also the exalted King of heaven, who rules the universe with an iron bar and a fist full of stars. All other heroes pale into insignificance next to Him. However, there are plenty of other men in the pages of Scripture who can also get the blood pumping and get faith levels rising.

Among my personal favourites are David's Mighty Men (*a.k.a.* **The Hard Corps**)—a platoon of elite soldiers who served their king with both devotion and distinction.

Their stories are hidden away in some of the more obscure pages of the Old Testament[2], yet these guys were the real deal. These men lived, loved and fought with such intensity that I defy any man to not be inspired by them. Such were their heroics they were rightly lauded as legends in their own lifetime, and even today they still have plenty to teach us about what it means to be true men of God.

The purpose of this book is therefore to spend time in the trenches with these incredible warriors. To study them, learn from them and better understand what makes them tick. We'll be meeting individual soldiers, going on mission with a special ops unit, and honouring the remarkable legacy that these great men left behind.

At the end of each encounter you will be given the opportunity to engage in a series of Combat Training sessions[3] that will further equip you to press on and fight as these men fought. Similarly, at the back of the book is the Armoury where you will discover a vast array of resources with which you can arm yourself for the battles that lie ahead.

My prayer is that by the time you've reached the end of this book, there will be no holding you back from launching into some serious, sanctified, no-holds-barred righteous ruckus for Jesus!

Man of God—It's time to put down the Popoids.

Welcome to *The Hard Corps*.

---

2 The two main passages that chart the adventures of David's Mighty Men are 2 Samuel 23 v 8-39 and 1 Chronicles 11 v 10-47. For the sake of simplicity we will be focussing mainly on the passage in 2 Samuel.

3 Combat Training sessions are great for individual study but are also perfect for groups of men who are wanting to get trained up and built together in the gospel.

CHAPTER 1

SET YOUR FACE

DEFYING THE ODDS WITH JOSHEB-BASSHEBETH
WARRIOR OF FAITH

"NEVER GIVE ME
THE ODDS."

HAN SOLO

Jason Bourne.
    James Bond.
        Jack Bauer.

How come so many action heroes own the initials JB? Whatever the reason I guarantee that the JB you're about to meet makes all those other guys look like *the Care Bears!*

> These are the names of the mighty men whom David had:
> Josheb-basshebeth a Tahchemonite; he was chief of the three...
>
> **2 Samuel 23 v 8**

Josheb-Basshebeth (JB) might sound like the sort of name that you'd only give to a child if you lost a bet or were high on drugs, but trust me—no-one ever made fun of this guy! JB was King David's ultimate warrior and one of the hardest men in the whole Bible.

David had a huge army with literally hundreds of thousands of highly-skilled soldiers who would have laid down their lives for him in a heartbeat. As well as these regular troops, however, he also had *The Hard Corps*—an elite squad of military specialists whose loyalty and warcraft was unparalleled. These Mighty Men were divided into two units: the Thirty and the Three. While the Thirty were exceptional, the Three were sensational! These three warriors were the cream of the corps—the best of the best!

And JB wasn't just one of the Three—he was the chief!

You could have searched the world over for a more gifted and more respected soldier but you would have never found one. JB was simply that good! You don't get to be one of the Three, let alone the boss, unless you've proved your worth on the battlefield.

Soldiers have always had to earn their stripes. So what exactly had JB done to get promoted to this position of honour? No doubt he had fought faithfully and courageously at the king's side on countless occasions and played his part in winning numerous battles. However, the Bible records none of those things. It focuses on one particular feat that illustrates perfectly just why he claimed the status as the number One of the Three. If you liked the film *300*—you're going to love this:

> He wielded his spear against eight hundred whom he killed at one time.   **verse 8**

JB took out 800 enemy soldiers in one epic stand-off.

ON HIS OWN!!!

That's incredible—*simple as.*

We don't know whether they all jumped him together and got wiped out in one mass rumble, or whether he had them form a line and took them out one by one. Either way you've got to admit that it's impressive.

And don't forget this wasn't a modern soldier armed with an assault rifle and hand-grenades—JB pulled this off with a single spear! Basically, he was a soldier like no other, who stood strong, fought ferociously and overcame impossible odds to win a victory that still causes jaws to drop today!

Now I appreciate that we don't often find ourselves surrounded by legions of heavily-armed, bloodthirsty warriors whose sole purpose is to bring an abrupt and brutal end to our lives, so what exactly can we learn from the example of Josheb-basshebeth? Why did God cause his story to be written down for us to read 3000 years later?

Maybe He wants us to be men who, like JB, defy the odds.

Defy the odds

When it comes to facing overwhelming odds I am something of an expert. As a father of four beautifully bonkers kids[1] I am permanently outnumbered! The Hankey horde love nothing more than ganging up on me, wrestling me to the ground and proceeding to batter me with whatever weapons they can lay their hands on—cushions, toys, furniture, the dog... There are no rules and there is certainly no mercy! They may just be kids, but there's a LOT of them![2]

Truth is, I never stand a chance.

That might be a light-hearted illustration, but let's not kid ourselves—as Christian men who love Jesus and are committed to doing life His way, we are seriously outnumbered! Forget odds of 4:1 or even 800:1, it can sometimes feel as if the whole world is against us. Everywhere we turn we are confronted by a culture that is fundamentally opposed to the cause of Christ, and as Christians we are in the minority.

As Christian men we are even more marginalised—we're even outnumbered in church!

When I played for our local football team I was the only Christian in the changing room—relentlessly bombarded by tales of drunkenness, crime and sexual conquest. As a club DJ I constantly felt like the only person in the venue who wasn't mashed off my face on pills.

I'm fully aware that, as you read this, you may well be the

---

1 At the time of writing I have a 5-year old, a 3-year old and a crazy pair of 1s!

2 Without doubt their most savage tactic is the "stinky face". This involves pinning me down on the floor and inciting one of the twins with a freshly soiled nappy to sit on my face and wiggle around. It's nothing short of domestic terrorism!

only follower of Jesus in your workplace, school, college, hall of residence, sports team, family or community. I know first-hand how hard it can be to stand up and be counted in such circumstances, let alone feel that you're making any kind of difference. To rep for Jesus these days you need to be a full-on gospel renegade, adopting a lifestyle of radical cultural defiance. Alice Cooper was spot-on when he said:

> *"Drinking beer is easy. Trashing your hotel room is easy. But being a Christian, that's a tough call. That's real rebellion."*

Which is why I'm so inspired by JB.

As I read it, when JB came face to face with 800 savage opponents, there were only three options available to him:
1. He could run away and hide.
2. He could drop his weapon and surrender, or
3. He could take a deep breath, tighten his grip on his spear and charge full-force into the face of adversity!

When it comes to living for Jesus, we are faced with the same three options today.

1. Cowardice
We could just turn our backs on the carnage of the battlefield and beat a hasty retreat to the "safety" of our cosy Christian bubbles, drowning out the sound of the horrors of war by singing soppy love songs to Jesus.

Sadly, there are many in our churches who take this option—comfort over combat. But this is not what soldiers of Christ are called to do. We were enlisted into the army of the King to be soldiers who stand and fight in the name of Jesus, not to cower in the shadows like a bunch of weak-kneed pansies!

God gave us a spirit not of fear but of power and love and self-control.

2 Timothy 1 v 7

Man of God—you were NOT called to be cowards.

You were called to fight!

2. Compromise

Alternatively, if the thought of pain, hard work and spilling blood on your clothes really doesn't appeal to you, there's always option 2. This is to surrender to the advancing army before a single blow has been struck— if you can't beat them, join them!

Tragically, this is the option that far too many Christian men are opting for these days. It simply involves rejecting the costly life of faith and bowing to the pressure to go along with whatever everyone else is doing! Fast-living, tough-talking, hard-drinking, fist-swinging, womanising, wealth-worshipping, porn-obsessed men have no place in the ranks of the army of Christ.

But as for you, O man of God, flee these things. Pursue right-eousness, godliness, faith, love, steadfastness, gentleness. Fight the good fight of the faith.

1 Timothy 6 v 11-12

Man of God— you were NOT called to compromise.

You were called to fight!

3. Combat

Clearly neither cowardice nor compromise were in JB's vocabulary. He was only ever going to take option 3—stepping up to the plate and doing what he did best—letting loose and kicking butt! And if we're honest we can't help but be inspired by the guts he showed and the stand he took.

However, there is a huge difference between applauding the heroics of King David's mightiest warrior and actually following in his footsteps! I mean how on earth do we actually stand and fight like that in our own context today?

Perhaps we need to stop the testosterone pumping for just a moment and come back to reality. The bottom line is this— *in ourselves we haven't got what it takes to stand.*

As men we don't like to admit this, but it is the raw truth. All of us at some point have crumbled in the heat of conflict and are painfully aware of our failure to fight and prevail. You might even be reading this right now and feeling a deep sense of shame as you recall your own moments of weakness and defeat.

I wish I could write as a man who has only ever stood strong against all odds as a faithful soldier of Christ. But I can't. I could put on a mask and make out like I've never joined in with inappropriate banter, that I've never been guilty of the lustful second glance, that I've never come home after an evening out with the boys gutted that I'd dishonoured Jesus and blown my witness (again). But it would be fake.

Truth is, I write as a man who, like you, has a chunky back-catalogue of sin and disgrace.

I'll share more about my past and the grace that rescued me from it in a later chapter. For now, let's just agree that as men we need to be more than just inspired to live for Jesus.

We need to be empowered!

JB's secret

So what was JB's secret? Where did his power come from? While it might be tempting to attribute his great achievements on the battlefield to his remarkable bravery, military skill or physical stature, I believe that his power came from a quite different source.

His secret was God.

JB clearly loved his king and fought faithfully for him.

And when you fight for King David, you fight for David's King!

David was a man whose heart was captivated by his King. A man who was both gripped and moved by the super power of God's Spirit. A man to whom God had promised great victory and immense blessing. A man who rolled with the Almighty and was so sure of his presence with him that it made him feel invincible. If you need convincing of that, check out these lyrics that David wrote:

> For by you I can run against a troop, and by my God I can leap over a wall.
>
> **2 Samuel 22 v 30**

Simply knowing that God was fighting both *with* him and *for* him made him bold enough to take on an entire troop single-handedly (and bust a bit of *parkour*[3] on the way home too!) That's because David was more focused on God's superior power, than the comparatively inferior threat posed by those who stood against him. Furthermore, David held firm to God's promises. God had promised him success. David fought like it was true!

> David had success in all his undertakings, for the LORD was with him.
>
> **1 Samuel 18 v 14**

By lining up alongside King David, JB was aligning him-

---

3 *Parkour* is that thing where guys leap over walls and through windows—like Daniel Craig as another JB—James Bond—in the opening scene of the movie *Casino Royale*.

self with the God of the universe. And when God's on your team—the odds look totally different:

> *800:1 = certain death.*
> *800:1 + God = no contest!*

It's all about perspective.

If we look to our own strength and abilities to stand, we'll soon be found wanting and get annihilated in no time. Similarly, if we focus on the ruckus that rages all around us, we'll quickly freak out and give up!

However, if we look beyond those things that are set *against* us—and fix our gaze on the awesome God who is *for* us—it changes everything. Paul calls this *"walking by faith and not by sight"* (2 Corinthians 5 v 7).

Just stop for a minute and remember again who it is that's on our team:

the LORD is with me as a dread warrior...

Dread warrior has got to go down as one of the most awesome descriptions of God in the whole of Scripture. And check out the dread warrior in action:

The LORD goes out like a mighty man,
like a man of war he stirs up his zeal;
he cries out, he shouts aloud,
he shows himself mighty against his foes.

Isaiah 42 v 13

God is ROCK HARD!

He's immortal, immense, unrivaled and unstoppable!

This mighty warrior is none other than King Jesus himself—the one who set His face to crush sin and Satan on the cross, before rising from the dead and obliterating the greatest enemy of all—death itself. Because of what Jesus has done, the battle is already won:

Thanks be to God, who gives us the victory through our Lord Jesus Christ.

1 Corinthians 15 v 57

Men who *don't* look to Jesus will always face defeat, whereas men who are fixated by Jesus fight like they're unbeatable— because they are!

Jesus is the One who fought for king David.

He's the One who fought for JB.

He's the One who fights for us.

That's a phenomenal truth! Jesus doesn't just *make* the difference, *he **is** the difference*.

So what?

If the example of Josheb-basshebeth has given you a fresh desire to man up and step up for your King, to defy all odds and do great exploits in His name—you need to be *sharpening your faith, not your spear!* You need to look to Jesus and see Him as greater than anyone or anything that stands in your way.

If you feel unworthy to fight due to past failures or indwelling weaknesses—you need to come back to the cross and see Jesus laying the smack-down on ALL your sin, setting you free to fight another day!

If you're feeling overwhelmed, under-resourced, outflanked and out-gunned, remember that:

The Spirit of him who raised Jesus from the dead dwells in you.

Romans 8 v 11

There is now a power at work within you that is more than a match for whoever and whatever decides to get in your face and try to back you down.

Man of God, you've been commissioned, empowered and unleashed to fight the good fight of faith.

It's time to grip your spear, grit your teeth and go for it!

If God is for us, who can be against us?
Romans 8 v 31

COMBAT TRAINING

Session 1
Growing as a warrior of faith

I hope the exploits of JB have inspired you to be a faith-filled gospel soldier who fights and prevails against all odds. However, it would be dangerous to look to JB alone for our inspiration. There was another warrior whose against-all-odds victory should do far more to encourage our hearts, strengthen our resolve and increase our faith. His name is Jesus, and when Jesus sets His mind on something, nothing and no one can stand in His way!

Read Luke 9 v 51-56

> When the days drew near for him to be taken up, he set his face to go to Jerusalem. And he sent messengers ahead of him, who went and entered a village of the Samaritans, to make preparations for him. But the people did not receive him, because his face was set toward Jerusalem. And when his disciples James and John saw it, they said, "Lord, do you want us to tell fire to come down from heaven and consume them?" But he turned and rebuked them. And they went on to another village." **Luke 9 v 51-56**

» *What was waiting for Jesus in Jerusalem?*

» What does it mean that Jesus "set his face" to go there?

» Why was Jesus rejected by the Samaritan villagers?

» Have you ever been rejected/belittled/opposed for following Jesus? In what way(s)?

» As a disciple you are called to deny yourself, take up our cross and follow Jesus (Mark 8 v 34-36). In what way(s) can you follow the example of Jesus to set your face to fight and to prevail?

Read Romans 8:
(it's big and chunky but totally worth it!)
After 30 verses of mind-blowing gospel truth, verse 31 asks a simple question: "If God is for us, who can be against us?"

» What's your answer to that question?

» Which of the epic truths and promises unpacked in this chapter get your blood pumping, your faith rising and your heart set on following Jesus, whatever the cost?

» What are you going to do this week to set your face, overcome the odds and stand for Jesus?

CHAPTER 2

STRENGTHEN YOUR GRIP

ON THE FRONTLINE WITH ELEAZAR
WARRIOR OF THE WORD

"IF THERE IS NO BLOOD
ON YOUR KILT YOU'RE
ONLY A DANCER."

SCOTTISH PROVERB

Question: What happens to the kid whose dad was named after a soon-to-be-extinct giant bird and whose granddad had a name that only donkeys could pronounce?

Answer: He grows up to become an Old Testament Samurai legend with a razor-sharp blade and a freakishly strong grip!

Gentlemen, it is my privilege and pleasure to introduce you to the swashbuckling number two of the Three. Mr. Deputy Dog himself—Eleazar—*the white-knuckled warrior:*

> And next to [JB] among the three mighty men was Eleazar the son of Dodo, son of Ahohi. He was with David when they defied the Philistines who were gathered there for battle, and the men of Israel withdrew. He rose and struck down the Philistines until his hand was weary, and his hand clung to the sword. And the LORD brought about a great victory that day, and the men returned after him only to strip the slain.
>
> **2 Samuel 23 v 9-10**

This incredible episode of courage and swordsmanship pretty much speaks for itself. However, before we start unpacking what we can learn from Eleazar's remarkable royal rumble, let's take a bit of time to set the scene and get our heads around exactly what was going on here.

First, it all began as a pretty standard battle situation—King David and his posse on one side, the Philistine army on the other. The Philistines were in every sense the sworn enemies of God and His people, so when the ruckus kicked off between these two armies, there was always a lot more at stake than turf and bragging rights.

The stage is set for the army of Israel to stand and fight for their beloved king, but as kick-off approaches and the soldiers start staring each other down, fear grips the hearts of David's men and they totally freak out.

Whether they gingerly slunk away into the shadows, or legged it home to their mothers for a cuddle and a mug of cocoa we're not told. What is clear, however, is that when the moment came to step up and fight, David's men chose to shrink back and cower... except for this one guy.

> and the men of Israel withdrew. [Eleazar] rose and struck down the Philistines. **verse 10**

We don't know how many he was up against, but the skirmish was clearly long and intense as, by the time the last Philistine had fallen, Eleazar couldn't even let go of his sword. The image of this heroic warrior standing victoriously over a multitude of vanquished foes, his trusty sword still clenched in a trembling, vice-like fist, is both breathtaking and compelling. Crucially, however, we can still learn so much from Eleazar today.

Ready for war

Eleazar knew exactly what he was up against:

> the Philistines ... were gathered there for battle **verse 9**

Enemy troops were on the warpath and they were thirsty for his blood. Eleazar knew this and he was ready.

We should be too.

Man of God, you need to understand that when Jesus

saved you, you were instantly drafted into the ranks of the army of Christ. His arch enemy, Satan, is now your enemy too, and as one of the King's soldiers you are engaged in the epic war to end all wars:

For we do not wrestle against flesh and blood, but against the rulers, against the authorities, against the cosmic powers over this present darkness, against the spiritual forces of evil in the heavenly places.

Ephesians 6 v 12

This is a bigger and far more brutal campaign than anything David's Mighty Men were ever involved in. This is a spiritual conflict with eternal consequences, and your enemy takes no prisoners.

He is a cunning, skillful, ruthless adversary whose sick lust for destruction will never be satisfied. He is the embodiment of sheer evil, and while we rightfully celebrate Jesus' devastating cross and resurrection combo that ultimately sealed his fate, we can't afford to get complacent.

Yes, victory is assured, but until our King returns to sort things out once and for all, the battle rages on—and it's intense:

Woe to the earth and the sea, because the devil has gone down to you! He is filled with fury, because he knows that his time is short.

Revelation 12 v 12, NIV

Be under no illusions—Satan is for real, he's vexed, and like a wounded animal backed into a corner, he ain't going down without a fight. He hates you like he hates Jesus and he is bringing the war to your door. His warcraft, however, is far more subtle than that employed by the Philistines.

He'll come at you with lies that unsettle the mind and

temptations that seduce the flesh. That might not sound like a particularly fearsome arsenal, but these are Satan's weapons of choice— and he's lethal with them! (Check out the way he infiltrated and obliterated humanity in Genesis 3).

So, unlike Eleazar, you may not have to hack your way through legions of Philistine thugs to go about your business today, but you can rest assured that as a soldier of Christ you will encounter savage, relentless opposition from your enemy. Whether it comes in the form of nagging doubts, an identity crisis, haunting memories from the past, the constant "need" to prove yourself, or the lure of illicit sexual activity, you can be sure that the enemy has got you locked firmly in his sights, and he's hell-bent on taking you down.

Many Christians believe that when they are tempted it must be because they are either wicked, weak, or both, but that's simply not true! Facing temptation is neither sinful or unusual. **It is absolutely normal**—*so get used to it!*

Tragically, however, Christian men are dropping like flies, apparently powerless against the forces of hell that have been unleashed against them. Left, right and centre, men are wrecking families through adultery, perving over pornography, drifting into apathy, shackled by fear, seduced by materialism... the carnage is horrific!

Man of God—we need to know what we're up against!

And we need to be ready and able to fight back.

Armed and dangerous

The question is, how do we fight back?

How can we do any damage to *"cosmic powers"* and *"spiritual forces of evil"*? How do we *"abstain from the passions of the flesh, which wage war against your soul"*? (1 Peter 2 v 11) Well, spiritual combat requires spiritual weaponry and just like Eleazar stepped into the fray armed only with a sword, the great news is that just like him, we get to swing a blade too!

Take ... the sword of the Spirit, which is the word of God.

Ephesians 6 v 17

Real men carry Bibles!

This might come as a shock to you, but the *only* chance we've got of going toe to toe with the hordes of hell and living to tell about it, is by gripping up the Good Book and becoming a *bona fide*, black-belt Bible-basher!!

That doesn't mean you have to turn into the dude on the corner wearing white sports socks and open-toed sandals while hurling Holy Bible hand-grenades at passing shoppers. *But you DO need to be a Bible guy.*

I've lost count of the number of men I've met who have tried to justify their lack of biblical edge with this lame excuse: *"I'm not really a Bible person!"* That is seriously more insane than an unarmed soldier stepping into the middle of a war zone and saying: *"I'm not really a weapons kind of guy!"*

They'll be wiped out in seconds!

We need to be Bible guys! We need to believe that *"the word of God is living and active, sharper than any two-edged sword"* (Hebrews 4 v 12) and that no other weapon compares to it. We need to be confident that God's word is all we need, and that by bringing it to the battlefield we're wielding a weapon that can smash the enemy to bits:

For the weapons of our warfare are not of the flesh but have divine power to destroy strongholds.

2 Corinthians 10 v 4

Now, all this talk about smashing Satan up with the Scriptures might sound great in principle, but what does it actually look like in practice?

Just like Eleazar gave the men of Israel an emphatic master class in sword-handling, what better way to learn the art of gospel warfare than observing the Grand Master of the biblical blade, Jesus Christ?

The Gospels record that before Jesus ever preached a word or performed a miracle, He was Himself confronted by Satan, who proceeded to bombard Him with some seriously heavy artillery. For 40 days Jesus was literally tempted in EVERY SINGLE WAY that we are[1]. Incredibly, after Satan had hit him with everything he had, Jesus was still standing, morally pure and spiritually supreme!

How did He do it?

In short, He knew how to handle his Bible.

Each devious lie and sinister temptation was masterfully cut down with the word of God:

Whatever Satan threw at him, Jesus hit back with: *"It is written..."* (see Matthew 4 v 4, 7 and 10).

- » He employed divine Truth to diffuse demonic temptation.
- » He was armed to the teeth with Scripture and Satan had no answer.
- » By simply speaking out the Word of God, Jesus sent Satan packing.
  Wow!!!

As we wage war against temptation in our own lives, we should be encouraged that the *very same sword* that Jesus brandished is available to us today. The gospel is still all we need to bring to the battlefield and is more than enough to get the job done. That's because behind every temptation is a lie that, if believed, will weaken our defences, leaving us wide open to enemy attack and powerless to resist tempta-

---

1   Hebrews 4 v 15

tion. The word of God, however, is divine truth and it's this truth that exposes Satan's lies for what they are, giving us freedom and victory over sin and temptation.

Here are a few examples of how that might work out today:

The guilt-gripped porn addict, who each night falls prey to the lie that meaningful sexual satisfaction is just a click away, might feel utterly helpless as he plunges deeper into a world of twisted fantasy and emotional numbness. However, freedom will come when he takes his hand off the mouse (or whatever else it's grabbing) and lays hold of God's word, which shatters the lie that true fulfilment can be found anywhere other than Jesus, and that pornographic shame is unforgivable. Jesus said:

> "Blessed are those who hunger and thirst for righteousness, for they shall be satisfied."
>
> **Matthew 5 v 6**

> If we confess our sins, he is faithful and just to forgive us our sins and to cleanse us from all unrighteousness.
>
> **1 John 1 v 9**

The angry young man who was raised in an abusive, loveless home may well rage against the world, hating life and even himself because he can't cope with the pain of feeling unloved and unlovable. However, when he wraps his clenched fist around the sword of the Spirit, the enemy's cruel lies will soon crumble as God's liberating truth enters the fray. God says:

> "I have loved you with an everlasting love." **Jeremiah 31 v 3**

> For God so loved the world, that he gave his only Son, that
> whoever believes in him should not perish but have eternal life.
>
> **John 3 v 16**

The stressed-out businessman, pursuing success at all costs, could be driven by the lie that his identity and worth are measured by personal performance and achievement. However, pressure will subside and peace will come as the gospel reveals that he can do nothing to impress God; yet, in Christ, grace is freely available:

> For by grace you have been saved through faith. And this is not
> your own doing; it is the gift of God, not a result of works, so
> that no one may boast.   **Ephesians 2 v 8-9**

Stuck to his sword

In situations such as these, potentially destructive temptation can be resisted by exposing and ruthlessly demolishing Satan's lies with the truth of the gospel.

No gospel = no defence!

In my own experience, the vast majority of Bible verses that have meant the most to me over the years are those verses that have helped me in my darkest moments of extreme temptation and spiritual assault. This seems to be the case with most Christian men I know.

In light of this you have to wonder why so many of us are so quick to let go of the word, relying instead on our own strength and resources to combat temptation, often with little or no success. This is yet another way that Eleazar is such a fantastic example to us because, as he stepped into the heat of battle, *"his hand clung to the sword"* and there was no way he was going to let go.

In fact as the victory shout was raised, his sword was so tightly locked in his war-weary fist that he couldn't have let go if he had wanted to! We would do well to copy his example, because if we let go of the gospel, we're sitting ducks for the enemy. Like Eleazar, we need to be stuck to our sword. We need the same unyielding commitment to scripture as godly men such as R C Sproul who, when asked about how he intended to bow out of the good fight, offered this brilliant response:

"I'll retire when they pry my cold, dead fingers off of my Bible."

You've got to love that.

RC's going out with his boots on. Gripping the gospel to the very end!

Man of God, we need to stop playing games.

Because Satan's not!

We need to live as Paul encouraged the Philippians *"holding fast to the word of life"* (2 v 16). Not just owning a Bible, or memorising a few "life verses", but drilled, skilled and brutally effective, able to inflict grievous injury upon the powers of darkness as they come against us. Refusing under any circumstances to let go of the gospel or compromise it in any way.

No soldier in the heat of battle ever complained that he had received *too much* combat training. You can never be *too* prepared for war. Effective training requires considerable discipline and sacrifice. We would do well to consider this when it comes to the good fight. So whether we roll out of bed an hour earlier to get our heads into the word, listen to sermons in the car, hook up with a friend to chew over truth, or simply make sure we're at church each week—let's be committed to honing our Bible skills.[2]

Eleazar's blade was covered in blood, not dust.

His grip was unbreakably solid.

His gritty heroics rightly went down in history— and yet he didn't get the glory for it...

The real Hero

The evocative image of Eleazar's faithful hand clamped to the handle of his sword is promptly followed by these words:

And the LORD brought about a great victory that day.   **verse 10**

The sword might have been in Eleazar's hand, but make no mistake, *it was God who won the victory*. The recurring theme of Scripture is that while we all have a part to play in the good fight, ultimately the battle belongs to God alone. So when we win, it's really Him who wins and who deserves all the credit.

This is especially true when it comes to waging war with Scripture. God's word is effective because the One who it's all about has already won. We can only ever take our stand against Satan because Jesus has already smashed him on the cross.

He's the real hero!

The heroics of Eleazar should rightly impress us, but may it be King Jesus who truly inspires and equips us to be white-knuckled warriors in our generation.

And may He get all the glory for it.

Strippers *v* soldiers

While it would be great to leave this chapter on that high

---

2   There are some great resources for deepening your faith and developing your Bible skills profiled in the *Armoury* section at the back of the book.

note, the text doesn't allow us to do that. The account of Eleazar closes with these harrowing words:

...the men returned after him only to strip the slain.   **verse 10**

Of all the words recorded in Scripture about the exploits of the Hard Corps, this phrase haunts me the most.

We are presented with a graphic image of what becomes of men who let go. These are the same men who at one point stood shoulder-to-shoulder with Eleazar, but who chose to flee for cover rather than to fight for their king. Here, after Eleazar has stood alone, fought alone and won an astonishing victory alone, the men come skulking out from the shadows and return to the blood-soaked field of battle.

Why? To apologise to the king? To honour Eleazar's courage? No. To plunder the spoils of a war that they refused to be part of.

Shocking.

Shameless.

Scandalous.

This passage shows us that there are only two kinds of men in the ranks of the armies of Christ—strippers and soldiers. The cowardly and the courageous. Those who let go and those who hold fast.

I know which sort I want to be.

What about you?

All Scripture is breathed out by God and profitable for teaching, for reproof, for correction, and for training in righteousness, that the man of God may be complete, equipped for every good work.

2 Timothy 3 v 16-17

COMBAT TRAINING

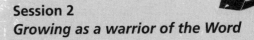

Session 2
Growing as a warrior of the Word

Eleazar fighting for his king with such ferocity that his hand literally cramps and clamps fast around the handle of his sword is a stunning story of courage and intense devotion. As men of God whose desire it is to fight for our King, it's important that we keep our grip on the weapon of our warfare—the sword of Holy Scripture. And who better to school us in the ways of the biblical blade than the King himself?

Read Luke 4 v 1-13

» *What do you learn about Satan's temptation tactics from this encounter?*

» *In what ways was Jesus tempted and how did He resist?*

» *What are the temptations that you battle against?*

» *What are the Scriptures that you can use to fight back with?*

» *Verse 13 says Satan departed "until an opportune*

time". He never quits. What can you do to keep your gospel blade sharp and your skills honed?

Read 2 Timothy 4 v 1-5
Paul wrote these words to his young apprentice, Timothy, as his life of full-on ministry and gospel adventure were coming to an end. He impresses upon Timothy the imperative to wield the sword of God's word.

» *What does it mean to "preach the Word" and why is it so important?*

» *Why is a firm grasp of God's word crucial if we are to obey Paul's command in verses 2 and 5?*

» *What is the ministry that God has given you to fight for? (v 5)*

» *What are you going to do to ensure that you fulfil it in the spirit of Eleazar, Jesus and Paul?*

CHAPTER 3

STAND YOUR GROUND

IN THE FIELD WITH SHAMMAH
WARRIOR OF PURPOSE

"U CAN'T TOUCH THIS!"

MC HAMMER

Martin Luther King Jr., a man tragically assassinated as he waged war on racism and fought for justice and equality, once famously stated that:

"If a man hasn't discovered something that he will die for, he isn't fit to live."

Read that again.

Those are powerful words. *Convicting words.*

As men we need a cause.

Thomas Carlyle rightly said that:

"The man without a purpose is like a ship without a rudder—a waif, a nothing, a no man. Have a purpose in life, and, having it, throw such strength of mind and muscle into your work as God has given you."

If you like the sound of that, then you're going to love our next hero. He's the third member of the Three, a formidable warrior who is buzzin' about beans and precious about his pods! Seriously, if you've got beef with this guy—it's game over!

Step up to the plate, Shammah...

And next to him was Shammah, the son of Agee the Hararite. The Philistines gathered together at Lehi, where there was a plot of ground full of lentils, and the men fled from the Philistines. But he took his stand in the midst of the plot and

defended it and struck down the Philistines, and the LORD
worked a great victory."

You can just imagine the headlines after this had gone down:
"Lentil Lover's Brutal Bean Field Blood-Bath!" Bizarrely, this
wasn't the first time that Lehi had witnessed such bloodshed.
Judges 15 records another gruesome encounter at Lehi when
Israel's hairy hit-man, Samson, single-handedly slaughtered
1,000 Philistines with the jaw-bone of an ass (a feat that I
used to think defied biological logic until I later learned that
"ass" was another word for donkey).

The Philistines and the Israelites clearly liked to rumble at
Lehi.

However, you've got to ask, what was this epic bean-field
battle really all about? Was this simply the action of a violent
vegetarian, or was there more going on? What could possibly
possess a man to put himself in harm's way and fight with
such tenacity for the sake of lentils?

Some say that, back in the day, lentils were a valuable com-
modity for trade. Others suggest that these particular lentils
would have been used to feed the armies of Israel and that
this was a strategic military strike by the Philistines. While
both of these opinions have merit, for what it's worth, I believe that there is a far more profound reason for why Shammah did what he did.

He understood that there was more than beans at stake.

These were God's beans!

This was God's country. The Promised Land. The nation
given by God to His people and from which the Saviour of
the world would eventually come. The field was loaded with
lentils because God had blessed this land and made it fruit-
ful.

This Philistine raiding party was seeking to take by force

what God Himself had given to His people. To obtain God's blessing by illegitimate means. To thwart the plans of God and snatch away the good gift of God's promise. That's cosmic treason! But that's what the enemy does:

"The thief comes only to steal and kill and destroy."

John 10 v 10

Man of God, if your desire is to live for your King, be under no illusion; the enemy is after you and his intention is clear—to steal, kill and destroy all that God has given you. FACT! That's why Shammah should be your role model right now.

Look again at what he did. While those around him fled, Shammah refused to back down. He had a cause much greater than himself to fight for and so he faced up to the Philistine bandits and did what was necessary to nullify their threat and defend the land.

Ultimately, it was the Lord's victory, though Shammah's strategy is still worth our attention.

He stood strong

My wife recently gave me a Welsh rugby jersey for my birthday. Printed in the collar is the phrase *"Dal dy dir"*, which means **"Hold your ground"**. It is there to inspire the Welsh team to defend valiantly and hold their ground at all costs.

In light of this, it is worth noting that Shammah's mission was a defensive one. This is significant as, while there are times for a soldier of Christ to go on the offensive (as we will discover in the next chapter), there are also occasions when standing your ground and holding your position are what counts. One of the greatest challenges of the Christian life is simply laying hold and keeping hold of that which God has blessed us with. To hold our position and stand strong.

This, the most significant victory of Shammah's glittering military career, was not a story of ground courageously taken, but rather one of territory successfully defended. We're told that Shammah stationed himself right at the heart of the bean field. He had no intention of taking ground from the Philistines; he was simply committed to digging his heels in and making sure that they kept their grubby mitts off his patch!

Shammah positioned himself in such a way that his enemies were left in no doubt that if they were going to take the beans—it would be over his dead body!

He defended defiantly

In this text, the word *"defended"* in Hebrew means to snatch back. As a dad of multiple kids I've witnessed the "snatchback" many times.

It normally starts with Child A wanting to play with a toy that is currently in the possession of Child B. Rather than waiting patiently or asking politely, Child A simply steps up to Child B and, with chilling, criminal precision, Child A will snatch the toy and make a run for it! Should Child B object (which is normally the case) they will then relentlessly pursue Child A and wrestle the toy back from their guilty grip with a defiant cry along the lines of *"Oi! Gimme that back!"*[1]

As funny as that may sound, it illustrates well what Shammah did. He literally snatched this bean field back out of the thieving grip of the Philistines with the same defiant *"Oi! Gimme that back!"* attitude.

He fought ferociously

No Philistines survived this encounter. It was literally a battle to the death. Shammah wasn't there as a diplomat or a me-

---

1   For the record my kids do have slightly more creative names than Child A, B, C etc.

diator. He was there as a warrior on guard, so when the enemy came to plunder, he took no prisoners. He fought with ferocious passion, and fierce intent. He fought like a man with a cause.

As we move on to consider those areas of our lives that the enemy has got locked in his sights, it's worth remembering the manner in which Shammah defended the King's beans.

» He was strong.
» He was defiant.
» He was ferocious.

So must we be.

Shammah *v* Jesus

When you stop and consider the gritty way in which Shammah battled for the bean field, it is striking how much similarity there is to the work of Christ in redeeming His people:

Shammah	Jesus
The Philistines besieged Lehi.	We were besieged by Satan, sin and death.
Defiantly held his ground at Lehi.	Defiantly sweat blood in Gethsemane.
Considered these beans a cause to fight and die for.	Considers us a cause to fight and die for.
Spilled Philistine blood as he snatched the beans out of the hands of thieves.	Shed His own blood as He snatched His people from the clutches of sin and death, delivering a fatal blow to Satan as He did so.
Was never going to let that field go.	Will never let us go (see John 10 v 28).

To follow the example of Shammah is actually to follow in the footsteps of Christ.

Battle for your beans

Clearly Shammah was driven by a cause much greater than lentil soup! His cause was his King, and he was driven by a passion for the purposes and the glory of God. What that meant on the ground, however, was that the seemingly small matter of a bean field became a cause to go to war. Why? Because God had given that land as a gift to His people to look after. Shammah was in every sense a steward of God's grace.

That's a high calling!

That's the calling that we ALL have as God's people. As men of God we have been given fields to fight for. Bean fields that become battlefields. We'll spend the rest of this chapter visiting a few of these fields:

Truth

Watch your life and doctrine closely.   **1 Timothy 4 v 16 NIV**

This is fighting talk! These were Paul's words as he charged his young protege, Timothy, to post armed guards at the gatehouse of his soul. Paul did this because he knew that, just like a rogue soldier, having infiltrated an army base, can unleash unimaginable carnage, *rogue theology* will do exactly the same to a man's life.

Fighting for sound doctrine and solid theology might not sound like the most glamorous of campaigns, but it's arguably *the most critical battle you will ever engage in* because as a man believes, so he is and so he lives.

It's been said that a man who stands for nothing will fall for anything. So if we want to be men who stand, we must ensure that it's the truth of the gospel that we're standing on, rather than the sinking sand of false doctrine.

» *What practical steps can you take to defend more vigilantly your soul and fortify your faith?*

Marriage

If God has blessed you with a wife, my plea to you is to fight *for* her, not *with* her.

As husbands, we are called to love our wives as Christ loved the church (Ephesians 5 v 25). That's a HUGE command. In fact, without grace it's impossible! However, just as Shammah was willing to put his life on the line for those lentils, we MUST be willing to lovingly, daily, lay our lives down for our wives—for their good and God's glory. I love what Carl Beech wrote on this:

> *"I see myself as the thorn on the rose, protecting the rose so that it can flourish and take the limelight. I am called to apologise first, take the hit and carry the can. I love my wife as Christ loved the church ... by dying to myself."[2]*

What do your decisions communicate to your wife about the quality of your love? Your use of time, money and technology? Your passions and pursuits? The way you treat her behind closed doors (especially the bedroom door)? Are you selfless or self-serving? Are you loving her like Christ?

» *Why don't you ask her?*

Children

I love being a dad, but it kinda freaks me out too. Dads have been given the awesome task of modelling God as Father to

---

2   www.carlbeech.com/carls-thoughts/real-men-aint-wimps—Read the whole post—it's quality!

our kids. That's a terrifying responsibility. Simply providing for their material needs doesn't cut it—even unbelievers do that (1 Timothy 5 v 8). Our kids need more than "stuff". They need Christ.

They need us to be reading the Bible to them, praying with them, loving them, listening to them, encouraging them, disciplining them, respecting them, laughing with them, enjoying them, wrestling with them (and letting them win), putting their interests before our own and loving their mother well. By doing so we commend the gospel to them.

We need to train our sons how to harness their strength, channel their aggression, master their testosterone, honour women, protect the weak and pursue their dreams for the glory of God. We must show our daughters what true, unconditional love looks like, encouraging them with cuddles, building them up with kind words and making sure that we hold the world record for telling them how beautiful they are.

» *Let's be fathers who fight faithfully and ferociously for the hearts of our kids.*

Sexuality

Your penis has the potential to get you into all sorts of trouble, if it hasn't already! The relentless onslaught of pornography, perversion and promiscuity has rendered many of us incapable of viewing women, and even other men, as image-bearers of God. Rather, we treat them as mere sex objects.

To view people through the warped lens of lust is to vandalise the artistry of God, yet that is what many of us are guilty of. In a filthy, fallen world, there is great need for godly warriors to stand up and fight for sexual purity. But how?

In Matthew 5 v 27-30, Jesus tells us that radical, brutal action is necessary. Even to gouge out eyes and chop off hands if that's what it takes!

Do you need to stop dating/groping/sleeping with (delete as appropriate) your girlfriend? Do you need to ditch your smart phone, get some accountability software on your computer[3] or even smash up your TV (which is fun, by the way)? Maybe making yourself accountable to your pastor or a trusted friend would also help.

» *As ambassadors of Christ we must be willing to do WHATEVER it takes to fight and prevail in the war for purity.*

Church

In the Garden of Eden God gave Adam the mandate to lead. He failed spectacularly, and as men we have been failing ever since. Nowhere is this more devastatingly obvious than in the church, where passionate, godly men are about as easy to find as a redneck with all his teeth!

The harsh truth is that the church is often weak because the men are weak. That's not a slur against my precious sisters in Christ. Rather, it's a challenge to the men of the church to step up to the plate and do what's in our DNA to do—be strong and take the lead.

As men of the gospel we should be:

» *contending for the gospel* (Jude 3)
» *aspiring to leadership* (1 Timothy 3 v 1-8)
» *modelling godliness in old age* (Titus 2 v 2)
» *exercising self-control in youth* (Titus 2 v 6)
» *praying like gospel warriors* (1 Timothy 2 v 8)
» *setting an example in ministry* (Philippians 2 v 25-30)
» *prophesying (proclaiming God's truth), dreaming dreams and casting vision* (Acts 2 v 16-18)

» *How do you measure up?*

---

3   Examples of good accountability software can be found in the Armoury on page 121.

Work

Men are hard-wired for hard work. However, since the curse of Genesis 3 all of our work inevitably involves pain, frustration, sweat and fatigue. Consequently, the desire to cut corners or throw in the towel is never far away.

So whether you're currently an employee holding down a job or a student grappling with your studies, the challenge is to press on and keep battling. Here's a couple of Scriptures to encourage you:

Work hard	"Go to the ant, O sluggard; consider her ways, and be wise." **Proverbs 6 v 6**
Work for the glory of God	"Whatever you do, work heartily, as for the Lord and not for men" **Colossians 3 v 23**
Work for the good of others	"Let the thief no longer steal, but rather let him labour, doing honest work with his own hands, so that he may have something to share with anyone in need." **Ephesians 4 v 28**
Work with integrity	"Unequal weights are an abomination to the LORD, and false scales are not good." **Proverbs 20 v 23**
Don't quit	"But you, take courage! Do not let your hands be weak, for your work shall be rewarded." **2 Chronicles 15 v 7**

If you haven't got a job—fight for one! I don't mean start swinging punches with other candidates at a job interview. I mean get out of bed, get serious, get out there and get trained up if you have to!

» *Make yourself the model employee.*

Justice

If we want to be men who accurately reflect the heart of God, we cannot and we *MUST NOT* remain unmoved by the plight of the destitute all around us. God loves the fatherless, the widow, the weak and the marginalised. His desire is for His people to burn with the same passion:

Open your mouth, judge righteously, defend the rights of the poor and needy.

Proverbs 31 v 8-9

A man who totally understood this was William Wilberforce, the British politician who, fought tirelessly for the abolition of slavery, a war he eventually won despite years of fierce opposition. He once famously declared:

"Let it not be said I was silent when they needed me."

There are many today who need us to step up and speak out. The homeless, the lonely, the refugee, the sex slave, the impoverished, the addicted, the afflicted, the abused, the persecuted...

» *Who is God calling you to fight for?*

Be watchful, stand firm in the faith, act like men, be strong.

1 Corinthians 16 v 13

COMBAT TRAINING

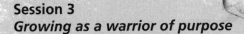

Session 3
Growing as a warrior of purpose

Hopefully the account of Shammah letting loose over a plot of lentils has got you in the mood to fight for your own field of beans—whatever that field may be. However, while Shammah's cause was indeed a noble one, it's got nothing on the great cause that Jesus came to fight and die for. If ever we needed inspiration to be men who fight for a cause greater than ourselves, it's Jesus we need to be turning to.

Read Luke 18 v 31-34

» *Jesus had a cause. What was it?[4]*

» *What cause(s) have you been given to fight for?*

» *What was it going to cost Jesus to fulfill His mission?*

» *Like Jesus, you are called to carry your cross.[5] What does that look/feel like on your mission in your context?*

» *Jesus' disciples clearly didn't get it, yet He still carried*

---

4   If you're stuck, check out Isaiah 53.

5   Mark 8 v 34-38

on. *Are there people who don't understand the cause you're fighting for and if so, what motivates you to press on?*

Read Ephesians 6 v 10-20[6]

Paul was on lock down in a Roman jail when he wrote this jewel of a letter to the church in Ephesus. Having laid out the gospel in the most dynamic and compelling terms, and urged the saints of Ephesus to live in light of that gospel, Paul closes out the letter by reminding them of the armour that God has provided for them in the fight.

» *Why do we need the armour of God? (v 11-12)*

» *Paul repeatedly commands us to "stand". What does that mean for you in your situation right now?*

» *How do the individual pieces of God's armour help us to hold fast and stand strong?*

» *How can we support and encourage one another to stand for Christ this week?*

---

6   If you're studying this as a group of 3 or more, it might be worth slicing it up and thinking carefully about each of the pieces of armour Paul describes..

CHAPTER 4

LOVE YOUR KING

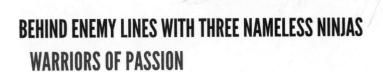

BEHIND ENEMY LINES WITH THREE NAMELESS NINJAS

WARRIORS OF PASSION

"FIGHT FOR THE HEART OF YOUR KING!"

JAMES DOUGLAS

So having met the Three, witnessed their heroism and marvelled at their military skill, it's now time to turn our attention to three new warriors. I'd love to introduce them to you by name but their identities remain anonymous—which only adds to their mystique. I refer to them as the Three Nameless Ninjas (3NN). Think of them as an elite squad of SAS commandos or Navy Seals who hail from among the ranks of the Thirty.

These guys epitomise passion, devotion and mind-blowing courage. You're going to love them:

> And three of the thirty chief men went down and came about harvest time to David at the cave of Adullam, when a band of Philistines was encamped in the Valley of Rephaim. David was then in the stronghold, and the garrison of the Philistines was then at Bethlehem.
>
> And David said longingly, "Oh, that someone would give me water to drink from the well of Bethlehem that is by the gate!" Then the three mighty men broke through the camp of the Philistines and drew water out of the well of Bethlehem that was by the gate and carried and brought it to David...
>
> **2 Samuel 23 v 13-15**

Unlike the passages we've read concerning each of the Three, this section reads much more like the script of an adventure story than a military case study. In light of this, it's worth our while to do a bit of background work as this will help us to better understand exactly what it was that inspired the 3NN to do what they did.

Captain Caveman

The opening verse is crucial as it sets the scene for the rest of the story. It introduces the 3NN arriving at David's home, though it would hardly have made it onto *MTV Cribs*!

At this stage, David is the anointed, but not-yet-appointed, future king of Israel and is on the run from King Saul, who wants him dead at all costs. He has set up camp in a vast expanse of elevated, rocky crags known as the cave of Adullam. This cave is one of my favourite places in the whole of Scripture. It might not have been a luxury pad, but the cave was, nonetheless, a place of remarkable grace. Check it out:

> David ... escaped to the cave of Adullam. And when his brothers and all his father's house heard it, they went down there to him. And everyone who was in distress, and everyone who was in debt, and everyone who was bitter in soul, gathered to him. And he became commander over them. And there were with him about four hundred men.
>
> **1 Samuel 22 v 1-2**

Like I said, Adullam's Cave was a remarkable place. The place where David had fled for sanctuary had become a place where many others were now running to for salvation. It was kind of like the Bat Cave, only it wasn't just the Caped Crusader and his loyal butler who knew about it. Word soon got round that "the cave" was the place to go if your life was a train-wreck and you had nowhere else to go. That there was a guy there who rolled with God, who had killed giants and who would one day be king.

This mountain-top maze of caverns would soon be home to 400 men (it must have stunk!) and would be the rallying point for David's most loyal and lethal warriors, not least the Mighty Men. At a time when the reigning king was a godless thug and the nation was going to the dogs, Adullam's Cave was Hope HQ.

However, let's not lose sight of the state of these men as they came to the cave. Every single man who arrived had this in common: *they were broken.* They were desperate. They had nothing to offer! They didn't strut into David's den with their heads held high, a heart full of courage and a fist full of faith. Rather they slunk in, their eyes to the ground, their hearts heavy and their hands empty. These weren't the stuff of legends. They were the scum of the earth. A shameful, pitiable, rag-tag gang of good-for-nothing nobodies.

Just the kind of gang, as it happens, that God loves to get His hands on to use for His glory!

What the men found at the cave wasn't comfort. It wasn't cash. It wasn't shallow words or empty promises. No. What they found was hope. A fresh start with a new identity. A brotherhood to belong to, and a captain worth fighting for.

He might not have been wearing a crown just yet, but in David, these men had found their king!

I take such heart from this story.

It's my story.

I am a man who was once distressed, indebted and bitter in soul. I found grace in the most unlikely place. Not in a cave, but at the cross!

Perhaps I should elaborate on that a bit.

As a young man I was relentlessly haunted by memories of past sins and regrets. I was plagued by guilt for many years and genuinely despised myself. However, rather than facing up to my past, I chose instead to run from it, which was as futile as trying to run away from my own shadow.

Frustrated and fatigued, I eventually ran out of places to hide and that's when Jesus stepped in. He showed me the cross, He blew my mind with epic grace and He kindly called me to follow Him.

I couldn't resist.

I came to Jesus humbly, empty-handed and broken-hearted, and He saved me. He wiped out my sin-debt and filled my soul with hope. He welcomed me into His band of blood-brothers, and gave me a cause to live and to fight for!

If you're a follower of Jesus—that's your story too!

I'm weeping as I write this because I forget it too often. But this is what God did for me. It's what He does. He redeems wretches and rebels, and raises them up as soldiers of salvation. In one of his letters, Paul lists the shameful ways of those who are outside the kingdom of God. He concludes with the words:

And such were some of you. But you were washed, you were sanctified, you were justified in the name of the Lord Jesus Christ and by the Spirit of our God.

1 Corinthians 6 v 11

Man of God, never forget where you came from. Every time you glance in the rear-view mirror and catch a glimpse of who you were BC, let it stir your heart to be deeply grateful to God for the saving grace of the gospel.

You might not be the man you want to be, but praise God—you're not the man you were!

Heart Cry

"I'd love to go horse-riding one day!"

Michelle had probably said it loads of times before, but this time I heard it. Personally, I'm not a big fan of riding horses. In fact I'd rather eat my own spleen than jump on the back of one of those bad boys! However, I love my wife to bits so when she expressed a desire to have a go—the light bulb went on and I booked us a horse-riding weekend for her birthday.

She loved it.

And to be honest, while it was one of the most uncomfortable and pant-wettingly frightening experiences of my life, I kind of enjoyed it too! But it wouldn't have happened if I hadn't been listening.

I share that story because it's reminiscent of what happens next. Shortly after the 3NN entered the cave they overheard their captain:

> "Oh, that someone would give me water to drink from the well of Bethlehem that is by the gate!" **verse 14**

Now this wasn't a command; it was a heart-cry. David was mindful that they were only 20 miles away from his hometown, Bethlehem, and with no Evian vending machine installed at the cave, his mind wandered back to his favourite watering hole back home.

Now I'm pretty sure that the 3NN didn't jump out of bed that day with the notion that a 40-mile round trip, including a small war, for the sake of a glass of water, was the best use of their time. But then they heard the heart of the king—and that changed everything!

There were as many as 400 men at the cave during this time, yet only three were close enough to their captain to hear the cry of his heart. That's significant because I am persuaded that one of the greatest sources of frustration among Christian men these days is this: *they know that they were born for an adventure but haven't got a clue what that adventure is meant to look like.* This is because they haven't heard the cry of their Captain's heart. Tragically, many then go seeking for thrills in all the wrong places, often with devastating consequences.

However, the problem isn't that God's not speaking.

The problem is that we're not close enough to listen!

Why is that?

In my experience men are generally pretty rubbish at relational stuff. We see it as girly business. That's why when we go to a church and are encouraged to *"greet the person next to you with a holy hug"*, or even worse, *"Let's all hold hands and pray"*, our instinctive response is: *"If this goes down—someone's going home in an ambulance!"*

We're just not like that. Men are not "touchy-feely". We're more "touch me and you die!" The truth is, however, that we were created and redeemed for relationships, both with God and with others.

> One thing have I asked of the LORD,
>   that will I seek after:
> that I may dwell in the house of the LORD
>   all the days of my life,
> to gaze upon the beauty of the LORD
>   and to inquire in his temple.
>
> **Psalm 27 v 4**

I have to confess that I struggle with the thought of gazing upon God's beauty. It's just not how I talk and, to be honest, it sounds a bit effeminate ... and soppy ... and weird. But do you know who wrote those lyrics? Not some pansy, pretty-boy worship leader, fresh from pressing his pants and putting product in his hair. No, it was David the giant-slaying captain of the caves. The ultimate warrior of worship. If the man after God's own heart was able to excel at both hand-to-hand combat AND heart-to-heart relationship, I guess it must be OK!

David craved an intimate relationship with his God. This in turn led to strong, meaningful relationships with his men. Like David, our King's not impressed by cold-blooded, dutiful obedience. Jesus is looking instead for hot-blooded, devoted disciples who desire nothing more than to be with Him. To enjoy His presence. To share His life. To hear His heart.

Man of God, how is your relationship with Jesus right now? If you can hear His heart, then you will know that it beats for mission.

Right now He's calling His people to go.

» To preach the gospel.
» To serve the broken.
» To combat injustice.
» To plant churches.
» To reach nations.

Is your pulse racing yet?

As soon as the 3NN heard David's heart, they couldn't hold themselves back. They simply were not content to stay hidden away in the relative safety of the cave any more. The king wanted a drink—they were going to be the ones to deliver. It's a compelling picture of what our response should be as men who love Jesus.

Stuff comfort.

Stuff the status quo.

Stuff what everyone else is doing.

Listen to the heart cry of the King and launch yourself into a life of unparalleled adventure.

Blood brothers

Before we move on with the story, there is an aspect of this mission that is worthy of special mention. Namely that *this is the only account of soldiers from the Hard Corps planning, fighting and triumphing **together***.

These men were determined to get the king a drink, but they were going to do it as a team. There is a crucial lesson for us here because as men we often lean towards the lone-ranger, maverick way of living for Jesus and this is neither healthy or biblical.

Scripture is packed with "one another" commands that are only possible in meaningful relationship with others. Furthermore, Proverbs 27 v 17 tells us that *"Iron sharpens iron, and one man sharpens another"*. It might be a bitter pill to swallow, but as men we need each other if we're going to thrive as soldiers of Christ.

As the old African proverb says:

> *"If you want to go quickly, go alone. If you want to go far, go together."*

That's why Wednesday night is the highlight of my week, because Wednesday night is *Fight Club* night. Fight Club is a dynamic ministry for the men of Hill City Church. Each week our band of brothers hooks up for a lock-in at the local gym. An intense training session is followed by an extended time of Bible study and prayer. We only have one rule: *"What happens in Fight Club stays in Fight Club!"*

Conversation is honest, frank, loving, brutal, provocative and fierce. We laugh, we confess sin, we grapple with truth, we encourage and we point each other to Christ. We literally wage war together. Don't get me wrong, sparks often fly— but that's what happens when iron sharpens iron!

I'm a better disciple, a better man, a better husband and a better father because of the brotherhood I enjoy with my Fight Club boys. I've got no doubt that the 3NN would have experienced the same as they served together on mission for the king.

Courageous passion

There was a series of TV adverts back in the day[1] that featured a dude in a dubious black polo neck who would dive off cliffs, swim with sharks, jump out of helicopters etc., all in the name of sneaking into ladies' bed chambers to deliver boxes of chocolate.

At the time I think he was meant to be a bit of a James Bond hero type. Looking back, however, he was blatantly just a lurker! Anyway, the advert always ended with the slogan: *"All because the lady loves Milk Tray"*. (For the record, I want to strongly advise you against *ever* creeping into a lady's bedroom, regardless of how much she might like chocolate, because you'll either be looking at a stretch in jail or death by stiletto!)

Hilariously, there are parallels between the actions of the Milk Tray man and the 3NN. Both went to extraordinary lengths, risking life and limb, all for the cause of delivering refreshments. You could even argue that both were motivated by love. However, the heroic love of the 3NN was far greater than that of the slightly creepy Milk Tray man, so perhaps we should leave the comparisons there.

Anyway, before we consider *why* the 3NN set out on this extraordinary mission, let's take a look at exactly *what* it was that they accomplished.

First up was the small matter of a 20-mile hike, probably under cover of night. This was a dangerous road, not least because there was a band of Philistines camped directly between them and their target. Did they choose the sneaky-soldier route and go around? No, they chose the kick-ass commando route and broke straight through the Philistine ranks with breathtaking courage and guile. They then had to locate the well, draw the water, bottle it and journey 20 miles

---

1   You can still find them on YouTube. Type in *Milk Tray Man* and enjoy the result!

back to the cave without losing it or spilling it or falling into enemy hands.

WOW!! *What an adventure.*

And all because the king loves Bethlehem H_2O!

There's so much that can be written about this incredible venture. Yet there is one thing about these three men that stands out above everything else: they *really* loved their king. And there is no greater motivator than love. If the stench of Adullam's cave served no other purpose, it reminded them of grace—that they were not the men they used to be. That they had been saved from shame and disgrace and that the only fitting response was to dedicate their lives to loyal service for their captain.

It was their love for David that drove them out of the cave and straight into harm's way. It was love that gave them courage to face up to and smash through overwhelming opposition, and love that gave them the endurance to see the mission through.

I love this because I see Jesus all over it.

Having been reminded of just how graced we are to be one of His soldiers... having been encouraged to draw close enough to Him that we can hear His heart cry for our lives—we are now given a compelling portrait of the power of love as a motivating force.

Man of God, never lose sight of who it is that you are serving. In Jesus we have a Captain who went before us, putting Himself in harm's way. He walked the brutal road to the cross, where He faced up to and smashed through the barrier of our sin, jail-breaking us out of the kingdom of darkness and faithfully delivering us into His kingdom of light!

Why? Because He loved us!

"We love because he first loved us."   **1 John 4 v 19**

The Christian life should simply be one of grateful response for the gospel.

Even when you were the baddest, maddest, murkiest and most messed-up sinner in town (and you were!), remember that your King loved you with such intense, unstoppable passion that hell itself couldn't keep you from His heart.

His rescue operation to the cross and back makes the 3NN's exploits look like a trip to the supermarket! If you have heard the cry of God's heart to go and to do great exploits in His name, then despite the danger and regardless of the cost, let the irresistible love of Jesus ignite in your heart an inferno of courageous passion for Him and for His glory.

Blessed beyond measure

So the 3NN make it back, flask in hand, and present it to their beloved captain. However, the drama doesn't end there. If I was responsible for writing the script for this closing scene here, I would have David and the 3NN together in the cave, surrounded by the 400. David would slowly raise the flask in a toast to these three heroes, then put it to his parched lips and swig it down with delight written all over his face.

But that's not how it ends. Read the story in full...

And David said longingly, "Oh, that someone would give me water to drink from the well of Bethlehem that is by the gate!" Then the three mighty men broke through the camp of the Philistines and drew water out of the well of Bethlehem that was by the gate and carried and brought it to David. But he would not drink of it.

He poured it out to the LORD and said, *"Far be it from me, O LORD, that I should do this. Shall I drink the blood of the men who went at the risk of their lives?"* Therefore he would not drink it. These things the three mighty men did."

2 Samuel 23 v 15-17

Instead, he refuses to even take a sip... and then tips it out all over the floor!

What?!! You've got to be kidding. After everything those men went through! What a waste!

Right?

Wrong!

The end of the story is the most passionate and profound part of the whole saga. The key to understanding what David was doing is the phrase: *"He poured it out before the LORD"*. David accepted the gift from his men and used it for something far more precious. He held in his hand a flask of Bethlehem's finest, a drink that his heart had so deeply craved, and brought to him by men whose courageous love was too much for him to handle. David was literally blessed beyond measure *and the overflow was worship.*

There was no more noble use for that drink than this. As David poured it out as a drink offering, far from devaluing the actions of his men, he was adding unprecedented value to what they did. The three warriors would not have been angered by David's response. Rather, they would have been blown away by the gesture. They would have seen that their acts of sincere devotion here on earth had eternal significance. They had looked to honour their king. Their king had taken their gift and given the praise and glory to their one true King in heaven.

What an inspiring thought, that the things that we do here on earth can somehow bless the heart of God in heaven. That what we do in this life is of eternal significance. Man of God, may that fill you with fresh courage as the heart-cry of your King propels you into a life of courageous passion and gospel adventure for His glory.

The love of Christ compels us...
2 Corinthians 5 v 4 NKJV

COMBAT TRAINING

Session 4
Growing as a warrior of passion

No question about it—the Three Nameless Ninjas were epic! It's impossible not to get energised and adrenalised by adventures like theirs. But stories of passion-fuelled exploits are not confined to the mighty men of the Old Testament. Our great King Jesus was a warrior of passion like none other. It's a mistake to think of Him as a mere Galilean carpenter, preacher and miracle worker. Jesus exemplified courageous passion like no one else who has ever lived—like the day He smashed up the temple with a whip ...

Read John 2 v 13-17

» *Why do you think Jesus was angry about what He found in the temple?*

» *What do you think about what Jesus does next?*

» *Does what went down at the temple change the way you think of Jesus? If so, in what way(s)?*

» *Jesus' temple rampage happened because he was "consumed" with zeal. What are you zealous about?*

» *No one can accuse Jesus of being all passion and no action! What steps can you take to put your passion into action?*

Read Matthew 28 v 16-20

The passion of Jesus took Him on a mission that led all the way to death on a cross. By rising three days later Jesus secured salvation for His people and His mission was accomplished. However, for His people, the mission was only just beginning. Shortly before hitching a ride back to heaven on the cloud escalator, Jesus gathered His boys together on top of a mountain and told them it was their turn to step up:

» *How do you think the disciples would have felt about being deployed on this mission?*

» *What would have given them courage?*

» *This "Great Commission" is still in operation today and we are privileged to be part of it. Where are you at with your role in the mission?*

» *The Three Nameless Ninjas were a pretty fearsome team and were irresistible as a unit on mission together. Who are the men/brothers/co-warriors that you can turn to, trust and fight alongside? How can you better train, fight and win together?*

CHAPTER 5

KNOW YOUR PLACE

STAYING IN RANK ALONGSIDE ABISHAI
WARRIOR OF HUMILITY

"IT'S HARD TO BE HUMBLE, WHEN YOU'RE AS GREAT AS I AM."

MUHAMMAD ALI

Ole Gunnar Solskjaer is one of the greatest players in Premier League soccer history. *"The baby-faced assassin"* played for Manchester United between 1996-2007, during which time he won a ton of silverware and scored 126 goals, including most famously the winning goal in the 1999 Champion's League Final.

However, Solskjaer is still remembered by many as the *"Super Sub"*, having scored 28 goals off the bench, a club record. For much of his career Solskjaer would look at the United team sheet and see his name below the likes of Beckham, Giggs and Van Nistelrooy and each time he had to resign himself to being on the bench yet again.

No one likes being benched yet Solskjaer never seemed to get vexed by it. There were no reports of training ground bust-ups or sulky transfer requests. He simply took it in his stride, kept fit and stayed focused, ready to step into action and give 110% whenever the gaffer gave him the nod. And he rarely disappointed!

Solskjaer exemplified loyalty. He clearly respected his manager, Alex Ferguson, and was willing to do whatever was asked of him to serve the best interests of the team. At a time when the only thing bigger than a Premier league footballer's salary was their ego, Solskjaer's attitude towards his manager, his team mates and his club was both humbling and inspiring!

Kinda like the member of the Hard Corps that we're going to meet next...

Make some noise for Abishai[1].

> Now Abishai, the brother of Joab, the son of Zeruiah, was chief
> of the thirty. And he wielded his spear against three hundred
> men and killed them and won a name beside the three. He was
> the most renowned of the thirty and became their commander,
> but he did not attain to the three.

2 Samuel 23 v 18-19

Of all the mighty men, I find Abishai the most intriguing.
Like Solskjaer, his resumé is impressive (he gets more press
in the pages of Scripture than any of the other mighty men).
Yet when I first encountered this fearsome platoon of war-
riors, Abishai was always the one whose name escaped me.
Whose military exploits I couldn't recall.

It sounds ridiculous when you consider that he was not
only Top Dog of the Thirty, he was also the most respected
soldier in their ranks. Yet somehow the others always out-
shone him. Perhaps it was because his section closes with the
words *"he did not attain to the three"*. This same phrase is also
attributed to Benaiah (who you'll meet in the next chapter),
yet it doesn't stand out as much in Benaiah's account, as a
considerable amount of coverage is also given to his many
acts of heroism. Certainly in this particular passage Abishai
is as much remembered for what he *did not* achieve as for
what he did.

That's humbling.

If you're a man who has known both the thrills of success and the pain of failure in equal measure, then Abishai
is your hero—a true warrior of gutsy humility. A man for
whom the good of the team and the honour of the king was

---

1 Not to be mistaken with Abishag—a sweet young lady who... er... got a job as King David's comfort blanket (1 Kings 1) and who surely tops the list of biblical names to *NEVER*
give your daughter!

of far greater value than personal glory. None of us want to be remembered as the man who didn't do this, or failed to do that. Yet that is precisely what Abishai's record states.

JB took out 800 enemy combatants: Abishai only managed 300. He *didn't* attain to the Three. Such a statement could easily be received as a kick to the teeth, especially when you add into the mix the potentially explosive element of male pride. You can just imagine the banter in the barracks

> *"Hey Ab, there's a Philistine crew outside ... looks like more than 300 though ... have you got JB's telephone number bro? Think we're gonna need some help on this one!"*

Yet Abishai just took it on the chin and got on with the task of doing what the king had given him to do.

» His job was to lead the 30, which he did with loyalty and distinction.
» He wasn't discouraged by the achievements of others.
» He wasn't distracted by delusions of grandeur.
» He was dedicated to his work.
» He was devoted to his king.

Because of this I believe that Abishai stands tall among the Hard Corps. According to author and pastor C J Mahaney, humility can be defined as "true greatness". If this is so, Abishai truly was great. It would therefore be worth our while hanging out with him to discover exactly what it was that made him tick.

To discover the secret of true greatness.

What's so special about humility?

Now you may be wondering why—after 4 chapters of meeting men who took on armies, waged war with intensity, fought for what matters and embarked on adventures for love of their king—we're now focusing on a man whose USP[2] is humility! Not very "manly" is it?! Well, all those other guys were indeed epic and, without doubt, the kind of men who rightly inspire us as soldiers of Christ. But Abishai reminds us that courage and warcraft are not all that matters in the good fight of faith.

Character counts too.

In our self-absorbed, glory-chasing culture, we are encouraged to pursue personal success at all costs. To idolise achievement. To demand recognition. To place value in status and significance. Whether in the world of business, the halls of academia, the sports club, the playground, the workplace, even within the family, the pressure to put ourselves first is real and it is relentless.

In our dog-eat-dog world, humility is a dirty word. It suggests weakness and lack of ambition. As men we would much rather be looked up to as strong, courageous and successful than looked down upon as humble. But God doesn't see things the same way. He's not impressed by soldiers with super skills but swelled heads. He's on the look-out for heroes of humility:

> But this is the one to whom I will look:
>   he who is humble and contrite in spirit
> and trembles at my word.

Isaiah 66 v 2

God is looking for humble men. Men who will lovingly serve Him and be faithful to give Him full credit for every victory. Men who don't have an inflated sense of their own importance, but are rather driven by a passion for the honour and

---

2   USP – Unique Selling Point

the glory of God. Men like John the Baptist, who said of Jesus: *"He must increase, but I must decrease."* (John 3 v 30)

So humility matters because God says it does. However, it also matters because to function without humility places you on a collision course with God: *"God opposes the proud, but gives grace to the humble"* (James 4 v 6). God won't share His glory with anyone, so rather than rolling with the proud, He resists them, and like a hedgehog going head-to-head with a truck, there's only going to be one winner! We pursue pride at our peril. However, if we want to be men who experience and enjoy God's gift of grace, then humility is the key.

I guess a helpful question to ask at this stage is: what the dickens is humility? In the interests of simplicity, we'll go with this definition from the Theological Dictionary of Dai: *"Humility is seeing yourself as God sees you."*

What does that look like in practice?

This is where Abishai can help us.

Humility puts success in perspective

As I mentioned earlier, Abishai had an impressive resumé. First, his family was one of unparalleled military pedigree. King David was his uncle and both of his brothers were war heroes, not least his brother, Joab, who was the commander in chief of the king's army. However, Abishai's reputation wasn't built on family connections alone; he was also a formidable warrior in his own right.

As well as starring in his own version of the movie *300*, Abishai played a pivotal role in numerous other military campaigns. It was Abishai who led the charge as Israel sensationally crushed 18,000 Edomites in Salt Valley (1 Chronicles 18 v 12-13). It was Abishai who, alongside David, crept into the camp of Saul, pleading for the opportunity to make a King Saul kebab:

> "God has given your enemy into your hand this day. Now please let me pin him to the earth with one stroke of the spear, and I will not strike him twice."

1 Samuel 26 v 8

David refused him. However, there is no question about what the most prestigious moment in Abishai's military career was. Abishai is the man who saved the king's life:

> There was war again between the Philistines and Israel, and David went down together with his servants, and they fought against the Philistines. And David grew weary. And Ishbi-benob, one of the descendants of the giants, whose spear weighed three hundred shekels of bronze, and who was armed with a new sword, thought to kill David. But Abishai the son of Zeruiah came to his aid and attacked the Philistine and killed him. Then David's men swore to him, "You shall no longer go out with us to battle, lest you quench the lamp of Israel."

2 Samuel 21 v 15-17

When you read stuff like that, you can see why Abishai was so respected by his comrades. But you can also understand why being known as the warrior who *didn't* attain to the Three could have been hard to take. He could have got in David's face and ranted:

> "Hey, where was JB when we slaughtered the Edomites? Why didn't Eleazar go into Saul's camp with you? Was it Shammah who stepped in and stopped you getting sliced and diced by that giant? No, it was Abishai! What recognition do I get? None. I don't give a stuff that I get a name alongside the Three—I demand a seat alongside them too. It's time to make space for me at the top table. It's time for the Three to become the Four!"

But that's not how it went down. Abishai was placed in charge of the Thirty. That was as high up the ladder as he got. No further promotions. No more responsibility. No greater recognition. The warrior who saved the king's neck and yet still *didn't* attain to the Three. Yet there is no record of Abishai dissenting or deserting. He fulfilled the duties required of him with due diligence and exemplary dignity.

That's humility.

In his letter to the Romans, Paul wrote these words:

> For by the grace given to me I say to everyone among you not to think of himself more highly than he ought to think, but to think with sober judgment, each according to the measure of faith that God has assigned. For as in one body we have many members, and the members do not all have the same function, so we, though many, are one body in Christ, and individually members one of another. Having gifts that differ according to the grace given to us, let us use them.
>
> **Romans 12 v 3-6**

Could it be that Abishai trusted his God-fearing king and accepted that he was better suited to leading the Thirty than joining the Three? Could it be that he had grasped the truth that there was a greater cause than writing his own story and seeking his own glory? Could it be that maybe, just maybe, he saw true success as having more to do with humble obedience and godly contentment, than acquiring trophies, accolades, plaudits and prominence?

WOW!!

> *That's humility.*
>> *That's the legacy of Abishai.*

Humility puts failure into perspective

At first glance, Abishai's military record looks pretty impressive. However, there's more to this soldier's story than first meets the eye. A lot more. As I mentioned earlier, Abishai knew his fair share of success and failure. And boy did he know failure?! If you're a man who is haunted by the shame of past mistakes and moments of weakness, you're in good company, as Scripture emphatically exposes Abishai as a messed-up sinner, just like you! We're going to look at two specific incidents.

The first happened as David and his men approached the village of Bahurim. One of Saul's relatives, Shimei, confronted David, hurling insults, rocks and dust at him as he entered the village. Abishai's response was immediate:

"Why should this dead dog curse my lord the king? Let me go over and cut off his head."

2 Samuel 16 v 9

Bit of an over-reaction really. Anyway, rather than impressing the king, David was enraged and rebuked him sharply for not recognising the sovereign hand of God in what was happening. Abishai clearly couldn't let it drop though, because three chapters later David again had to rebuke him for wanting to kill the same man for the same offence. When your beloved king twice exposes your sin and gives you a rollicking in front of others, the shame is great. Abishai would have felt it deeply.

However, Abishai's most disgraceful moment happened in 2 Samuel 3. Having seen their brother Asahel brutally murdered by Abner (Saul's cousin), Abishai and his brother Joab wasted no time in murdering their brother's assailant in cold blood. This horrified David, who cried out:

> Do you not know that a prince and a great man has fallen this day in Israel? These men, the sons of Zeruiah, are more severe than I. The LORD repay the evildoer according to his wickedness!

2 Samuel 3 v 38-39

Far from simply avenging his brother, Abishai had angered the king, who literally handed him over to God for judgement.

That's serious!

Make no mistake, Abishai might have been a prolific warrior, but he also knew moments of catastrophic failure. Which is why the fact that here, right at the end of David's reign, Abishai is still listed as one his mighty men, should give us hope. I mean let's face it, we're not unlike Abishai, are we? Sure, we might have known our fair share of "victories" as men of God, but we've also got a back-catalogue of shameful failures and mistakes.

Perhaps it's time for some raw honesty...

I've now been following Jesus for over half of my life and in that time I have done some wretched things. I have messed around sexually in multiple ways with multiple women, causing all manner of emotional and spiritual carnage. I've broken hearts, betrayed friends and destroyed relationships.

I have been smashed on alcohol more times than I can count and was once found unconscious in a pool of my own vomit outside a nightclub in Cardiff. I've abused my body in countless ways and now have arthritis and a permanent limp to show for it. I've watched all manner of filth on all sorts of screens. I've swung punches, hurled abuse, told countless lies and lived recklessly with no regard for anyone other than myself.

And that's just the stuff I've done that I shouldn't have.

There's also a shed-load of stuff that I should have done that I never did.

That's not me trying to sound like a bad-ass by the way. That's me trying to reassure you that you're not the only one who's got a list (I know you have!). In all honesty, I sometimes have to pinch myself and ask how did I ever become a faithful husband and a doting dad? How have I got so many friends who care about me? How have I ended up in a church that I love like family? How the chop-sticks did I ever become a *pastor*? Who am I even to contemplate writing a book about living as a godly man?

I'm a disgrace.

And I deserve nothing other than hell.

This is why I love Abishai, because more than any other member of the Hard Corps, I see a man who didn't only screw up *before* he met his king, but was still screwing up *after* joining his ranks too. A man like me! However, I also see the grace of God at work. The same grace that saved me, and continues to save me.

When you see Abishai in this light, all of a sudden the fact that he didn't attain to the Three seems quite trivial really. The fact that he was even allowed to be a foot soldier, let alone one of David's mighty men, let alone the chief of the Thirty, all speaks of the kindness of the king.

Benjamin Franklin said it well:

"After crosses and losses, men grow humbler and wiser."

Could it be that Abishai epitomised humility because, despite all the trophies of his glittering military career, he still saw himself as he really was—a trophy of amazing grace?

Humility with skin on

As encouraging as Abishai's example of humility is, it would be wrong to elevate him as the ultimate model of humility. If, like me, you feel stirred up to pursue humility and see both your successes and your failures in their true light, can I encourage you to look beyond the ranks of David's Mighty Men and to fix your gaze on Jesus Christ, the true King of humility.

Jesus is literally humility with skin on, and from His cosmic drop from the courts of heaven to the cattle trough of Bethlehem and all the way to the cross, His radical example of humility is compelling:

> Have this mind among yourselves, which is yours in Christ Jesus, who, though he was in the form of God, did not count equality with God a thing to be grasped, but emptied himself, by taking the form of a servant, being born in the likeness of men. And being found in human form, he humbled himself by becoming obedient to the point of death, even death on a cross.
>
> **Philippians 2 v 5-8**

At the cross, we see our most "impressive" accomplishments and greatest success stories for what they really are—filthy rags[3]. Similarly, we see the horrific, grim reality of our filthy history for what it is too—forgiven for ever![4] At the cross we see that our acceptance by God is not down to our successes nor jeopardised by our failures. Our acceptance comes by grace alone.

A soldier of Christ will be captivated by the cross and grateful for grace.

---

3 Isaiah 64 v 6 literally likens our most "righteous" acts to used tampons!

4 Isaiah 43 v 25 tells us that God forgives AND forgets.

A soldier of Christ will find true freedom as he sees himself as God sees him.

A soldier of Christ will do whatever his captain commands, regardless of cost and consequence.

Such is the way of Abishai.

> He has told you, O man, what is good;
> and what does the Lord require of you
> but to do justice, and to love kindness,
> and to walk humbly with your God?
>
> **Micah 6 v 8**

COMBAT TRAINING

Session 5
Growing as a warrior of humility

There is no doubt that Abishai is a warrior of great honour. After all, could there be a greater display of humble devotion than putting personal aspirations aside and faithfully serving the king in the way that Abishai did? Incredibly, yes! What about the King of kings exchanging the glory of heaven for the grit of this world? Stooping to our level not only to rub shoulders with us, but to seek and to serve sinners like us?! We serve a humble God, as Jesus proved so poignantly, shortly before His death when He stripped off, knelt down and washed all manner of faeces and filth from His disciples' feet:

Read John 13 v 1-20

» *Back in the day, washing feet was the role of the lowliest servants. What does this tell you about Jesus?*

» *He even washed Judas' feet. What does that tell you about Jesus?*

» *Why do you think Peter initially resisted Jesus?*

» *What caused him to change his mind and submit to the servant-hearted love of Jesus?*

» *In verse 15 Jesus makes it clear that His foot washing exercise was an example for us to follow. What would be an equivalent act of humble service in your cultural context?*

» *What's stopping you doing it?*

Read Philippians 2 v 1-11

Humility is a battle for any and every follower of Jesus because pride is hard-wired in us. When Paul wrote to the church in Philippi, he pleaded with them to combat their natural inclination to be proud by modelling the humility of Christ.

» *Where does the journey to humility start? (v 5)*

» *Verses 6-7 tell us that Jesus willingly loosened His grip on His "rights" as the Son of God. As you pursue humility, what are the things that you struggle to let go of?*

» *Jesus' humility took Him all the way from heaven to calvary. What practical steps can you take to kill your pride and follow Jesus' example of radical, sacrificial humility?*

CHAPTER 6

FACE YOUR FEARS

IN THE LINE OF FIRE WITH BENAIAH
WARRIOR OF COURAGE

"COURAGE IS BEING
SCARED TO DEATH ...BUT
SADDLING UP ANYWAY."

JOHN WAYNE

The Fantastic Four have got The Human Torch.
The Hard Corps have got Benaiah.

These dudes are definitely cut from the same cloth: wild, impetuous, hot-headed, but definitely fun to be around. You'd be forgiven for thinking that both these guys have got ADHD[1] as they live life in the fast lane, lusting after adventure and laughing in the face of danger. Fear doesn't paralyse these guys—it energises them!

Flame on!

Abishai was the member of the Hard Corps whose identity I kept forgetting. I had the opposite problem with Benaiah. This warrior for me was the most memorable and the most inspiring of the whole team. His profile in this passage is extensive, featuring three mind-blowing episodes, though it's neither the word count, nor the body count that most stands out in the case of Benaiah.

It's the crazy, almost comical nature of the battles that he fought. Such is the nature of his exploits you could almost think that they were borrowed from the realm of fantasy. However, that's where The Human Torch and Benaiah differ. The Torch is just a comic book hero, while Benaiah's life is not the stuff of fiction—this man was the real deal.

He really did live.

He really did do this stuff.

You really are gonna love him...

---

1   Contrary to popular belief, ADHD does not stand for 'A Dai Hankey Disorder'

> And Benaiah the son of Jehoiada was a valiant man of Kabzeel, a doer of great deeds. He struck down two ariels of Moab. He also went down and struck down a lion in a pit on a day when snow had fallen. And he struck down an Egyptian, a handsome man. The Egyptian had a spear in his hand, but Benaiah went down to him with a staff and snatched the spear out of the Egyptian's hand and killed him with his own spear. These things did Benaiah the son of Jehoiada, and won a name beside the three mighty men. He was renowned among the thirty, but he did not attain to the three. And David set him over his bodyguard.
>
> **2 Samuel 23 v 20-23**

OK, first thing to note is that his dad, Jehoida, is a priest. That essentially makes him a pastor's kid, and, in my experience, pastors' kids are often a bit bonkers. Benaiah definitely fits the bill on that score.

However, priest or not, his dad must have been buzzin' that his son had a reputation for being a "valiant man" and "a doer of great deeds." Those words would make any dad proud. Certainly, my prayer for my boys as they grow up is that rather than being known for shallow, sinful living, they would take after Benaiah and be respected for their good works.

We haven't even got to the action yet and already Benaiah is sounding like a legend. Each of these three epic encounters will only serve to prove that point. However, as we proceed, please be aware that rather than just admiring as spectators in the crowd, we're going to get up close and personal, stepping right into the line of fire alongside our hero. We're going to go eyeball to eyeball with two ferocious warriors, jump into a pit with a savage lion and go toe to toe with a heavily armed giant. As we do so, we're going to confront three very different fears that are all too common to us as men: fear of the unknown, fear of failure and fear of man. Benaiah will teach us how to fight and prevail against each of these as we learn to live life with radical faith and gutsy gospel intensity.

You up for it?

Good.

Seconds out...

Round 1: "Fear of the unknown"
Feat: *Two freaks from Moab*

First up for Benaiah are two "Ariels of Moab". Now I know what you're thinking, "what's a freakin' Ariel from Moab?"

This would actually be a very well-worded question because, ironically, these guys were freaks! In the original language "Ariel" is a very unusual word, so most Bible translations play safe and just stick with the word Ariel. The King James Version, however, is much braver, and introduces Benaiah's opponents as two "lion-like men". These guys are essentially a mutant hybrid of Moabite warrior and man-eating lion, a bit like the insane wrestling midgets from the movie *Nacho Libre* ... but a lot gnarlier!

In other words, Benaiah is about to take on a pair of fearsome freak terrorists—a tag-team contest that he never could have prepared for in a million years. One minute he's going about his daily business; the next he's confronted by two UFOs[2] who want to rip his face off.

That's gotta freak you out, right?

Now, Benaiah didn't wake up that day and think: *"I know, I'm gonna go and find myself a couple of freaks to annihilate!"* But those freaks were out there and eventually they found him. Believe it or not, this episode is not entirely different from what still confronts us today.

> » When the doctor told us that my wife was probably suffering a miscarriage—*it freaked me out.*

---

2   UFO—Unidentifiable Freaky Opponents.

- » When cancer got a grip on my mother, eventually killing her—*it freaked me out.*
- » When Christmas was approaching and we had no money for gifts—*it freaked me out.*
- » When God made it clear that He wanted me to uproot my family and plant a church on a notorious estate in the Welsh valleys—*it **totally** freaked me out.*

These were freak moments that I had never experienced before. I didn't go looking for them but they stepped up to me, and just like Benaiah didn't have a "How to handle an Arial of Moab" manual, I didn't have a "How to handle your mother dying" manual. I was totally freaked out, but by God's grace I came through it.

Man of God, there are still "lion-like men" roaming the streets today. Perhaps not physical freaks like these Moabites, but circumstances and situations that will rip you to shreds given half a chance.

You will get sick. People will die. Money will be tight. Relationships will break up. Your kids will rebel. Terrorists will strike again. These things *will* happen. The challenge for us as men is to not allow the fear of the unknown to cripple us, to back us into a corner. Rather, we need to be able to look that fear dead in the eye and then pulverise it Benaiah style.

How do we do that?

We find our courage in God's word:

For the righteous will never be moved; he will be remembered for ever. He is not afraid of bad news; his heart is firm, trusting in the LORD. His heart is steady; he will not be afraid, until he looks in triumph on his adversaries.

Psalm 112 v 6-8

We fight the fear of what *we don't know* with the power of *what we **do** know*:

> For **I am sure** that neither death nor life, nor angels nor rulers, nor things present nor things to come, nor powers, nor height nor depth, nor anything else in all creation, will be able to separate us from the love of God in Christ Jesus our Lord.
>
> **Romans 8 v 38-39**

I guarantee you that as you seek to fight the good fight of faith, somewhere down the line you will be ambushed by various UFOs, and you're going to get freaked out. The only way that you're going to live to tell about it is to arm yourself with the gospel:

> There is no fear in love, but perfect love casts out fear.
>
> **1 John 4 v 18**

When you come out swinging, with the perfect love of God pulsing through your veins and the unshakeable, empty-tomb assurance that Jesus has already won the war, the freaks don't stand a chance!

Round 2: "Fear of failure"
Feat: *A lion in a pit on a snowy day*

As we learned from Abishai, failure can be devastating. However, it's not only failure in the shameful things that we *do* (sinful action) that affects us. Sometimes it's our failure in the good things that we *didn't do* (sinful inaction) that cuts most deeply.

Those moments when you were presented with a God-given opportunity to step up, speak out or get involved for Him, but rather than grabbing it with both hands, you froze and the moment was lost...

- » A colleague asks you to tell him what this God stuff is all about, but you choke.
- » You're offered the chance to fill a gap in one of the ministries at church, but you drown out God's voice saying *"go"* with your own voice screaming *"no!"*
- » That person who was being mercilessly bullied really needed someone to step in and stick up for them, but you chose to *"mind your own business"* and stay out of it.

I can think of many such moments in my own life. Knowing that my God is both sovereign and gracious certainly takes the sting out of past regrets, but the reality is that I would have far fewer regrets in the first place if I had hooked up with Benaiah sooner.

Benaiah is the kind of guy that doesn't let the moment pass, but rather launches himself into God's purposes with such ferocious faith that at first glance it seems utterly reckless. The most famous example of this occurred on a cold, snowy day when Benaiah noticed a pit and then clocked that there was a lion trapped inside it. Now this is where Benaiah differs from the rest of us, because most ordinary mortals would see a hungry lion in a pit and think: *"Phew! Thank God he's stuck down there while I'm safe up here"*. Before legging it like Usain Bolt with his pants on fire.

But that's not Benaiah. Where others would see danger to be avoided at all costs, he senses an opportunity too good to be missed. So he takes a running jump and hurls himself headlong into his destiny—and the closest thing to a UFC Cage Fight you'll find in Scripture.

We're not given details of the battle, but it must have been intense. The snarling, slashing, sliding, raging, roaring and ripping would have been horrific. The result, however, would be that only one champion would emerge from that icy, blood-spattered snow pit. And on this occasion it wasn't the King of the Jungle, it was the valiant Big Cat Killer from Kabzeel.

Now you might think that for Benaiah to leap into a death match in a snowy pit with a 500lb man-eating beast, he must be nuttier than a squirrel's picnic. However, of all his incredible exploits, this is the one for which he is most famous.

Furthermore, Benaiah went on to be promoted as the head of David's bodyguard, and later as the commander in chief of all the armies of Israel. Would that have happened if he hadn't struck down the lion that day? Who knows? All I know is that if I'm looking for a bodyguard and there's a lion-killer in my ranks he's at least getting an interview!

Now, I don't think for a minute that Benaiah killed that lion purely to get promoted. I think he did what he did because he was the kind of man to run after lions rather than running away from them. Some men are like that. In fact Benaiah is not the only man in the Bible to prevail over a lion. He's in very good company:

» *Samson* ripped a lion to pieces with his bare hands when the Spirit rushed upon him (Judges 14 v 5-6).
» *David* used to grab lions by the beard and slaughter them when protecting his sheep, fully trusting that God was protecting him (1 Samuel 17 v 34-37).
» *Daniel* was defended by an angel in the lion's den because of his blameless character (Daniel 6 v 22).

When it comes to seizing the gospel opportunities that God places before us, we are far more likely to grab those moments by the scruff of the neck if we are consumed by the Spirit, trusting God and living with integrity. Men like that don't fail because all their strength and their confidence is in God alone. That's why Paul could say: *"I can do ALL things through him who strengthens me."* (Philippians 4 v 13)

» *Aren't you fed up with "safe" Christianity?* **I am.**

» *Aren't you stoked that Jesus didn't play it safe, but rather went all the way to the cross?* **I am!**

And I don't believe that Jesus saved us to be safe. I believe He saved us for a life of costly sacrifice and crazy leaps of faith. I believe that *"people who know their God shall be strong, and carry out great exploits"* (Daniel 11 v 32 NKJV). I believe that God has so much more for us than the bland, mediocre, tame brand of Christianity that we have accepted as the norm. I believe that it's time for men of faith to rise up and expose risk-free Christianity for what it really is—epic failure. It's time to stop running from lions and start brawling with them instead. To forcibly grab hold of what God's got for us and not let go of it.

Perhaps Benaiah did what he did because he served a lion-slaying king.

But then so do we!

Peter rightly warns us to be on our guard because *"the devil prowls around like a roaring lion, seeking someone to devour."* (1 Peter 5 v 8) But he then commands us to *"Resist him, firm in your faith…"* (1 Peter 5 v 9) Nothing should beef up our faith more than seeing Jesus trample that lion at the cross, then believing that we now have the authority to do the same:

You will tread on the lion and the adder; the young lion and the serpent you will trample underfoot.

Psalm 93 v 13

Our King is the ultimate lion slayer.

So next time destiny growls at you from the bottom of a snowy pit, don't freeze with fear, but look to your King, jump in and grab it with both hands.

Round 3: "Fear of man"
Feat: *The Egyptian giant*

Benaiah's king was no stranger to killing lions and he was no stranger to toppling giants either![3] With that in mind, let's meet Benaiah's final challenger, a good-looking chap from Egypt who, we discover in 1 Chronicles 11 v 23, was a whopping 7 $1/2$ foot giant and who brandished a spear that most ordinary men could barely lift. On top of all that, on this occasion Benaiah was armed only with a stick.

OK let's press "pause" there...

Benaiah doesn't stand a chance. Everything here is pointing towards certain death for our hero, who is out-sized and out-gunned. The stats don't lie—this Egyptian is in a totally different class. Perhaps Benaiah should just face facts, wave the white flag and go home for a cup of tea, but then I guess he's not like that, is he?

Right, hit "play" again...

Oh.

It's over already!

How in the world did Benaiah even get close to the giant, let alone wrestle that monstrous spear out of his vice-like fist and use it to kill him?

That's nuts.

No, that's Benaiah!

This particular rumble inspires me because Benaiah was confronted with an opponent *so formidable* that he should have surrendered on the spot. But he didn't. If this man was unable to strike fear into the heart of this warrior, no man could. I find that challenging because fear of man is some-

---

3   Check out 1 Samuel 17.

thing that I'm constantly battling against. Scripture teaches us that *"The fear of man lays a snare, but whoever trusts in the Lord is safe"* (Proverbs 29 v 25). Are you safe or snared right now? Here are a few tell-tale signs that you might be trapped by the fear of man:

» You keep quiet about Jesus for fear of being laughed at.
» You constantly compare yourself to others.
» You need other people's approval.
» You tend to follow the crowd.
» You fear rejection.
» You can't say no.

If that's you, it's time to break out and wage war on the fear of man.

It's time to slay a giant.

The solution to fearing man is not to focus less on those around you or to increase your own self esteem. No, what's needed is to replace the unhealthy fear of man with a healthy fear of God. To focus on His size, holiness, power and un-beatable love. When you see God as He truly is, suddenly everything and everyone else shrinks back to their proper size. King David illustrated this perfectly as he took out the most famous giant to ever walk the earth, Goliath of Gath:

"You come to me with a sword and with a spear and with a javelin, but I come to you in the name of the Lord of hosts, the God of the armies of Israel, whom you have defied. This day the Lord will deliver you into my hand, and I will strike you down and cut off your head. And I will give the dead bodies of the host of the Philistines this day to the birds of the air and to the wild beasts of the earth, that all the earth may know that there is a God in Israel, and that all this assembly may know that the Lord saves not with sword and spear. For the battle is the Lord's, and he will give you into our hand."

1 Samuel 17 v 45-47

David didn't focus on Goliath's colossal 12ft frame nor his devastating arsenal of weapons. David looked to the infinitely more terrifying Lord of hosts, and the rest is history.

Flame on!

As men of God we will only be rid of the fear of the unknown when our hearts are burning with the perfect love of God. We will only be free from fear of failure when our lives are fully surrendered to the victorious, all-conquering King of the cross. And we will only be liberated from the fear of man when our vision is dominated by the all-powerful God of the universe, who is infinitely greater than anything, everything and everyone else.

Freaks, lions, giants—bring 'em on.

Our God is greater.

Flame on!

Be strong and courageous. Do not be frightened, and do not be dismayed, for the LORD your God is with you wherever you go.

Joshua 1 v 9

COMBAT TRAINING

Session 6
Growing as a warrior of courage

So what more can be said about Benaiah, the freak-slaying, lion slaughtering, giant killer? Not much really—the man was a beast whose courage we can only marvel at. He certainly seemed to know how to put fear in its right place—something that all of us men need to learn. However, if we really want to learn the key to laying the smack down on fear, we need to observe the One who overcame fear of the very highest order—Jesus Christ.

Read Luke 22 v 39-46

» *Jesus knew that the time of His crucifixion was almost upon him. Why was that a terrifying thought?*

» *Have you ever known fear as you've followed Jesus? If so, in what way(s)?*

» *As He faced His fears, Jesus prayed. What does His prayer (v 42) tell you about His relationship with the Father?*

» *When the pressure got more intense, so did Jesus' prayer (v 44). What can you learn from His example here?*

» *What action can you take to deepen your prayer life,*

draw closer to the Father and overcome your fears as you submit to His will for your life?

Read Acts 4 v 1-31
After performing a famous miracle that saw a 40-year-old man able to walk for the first time in his life, Peter and John were arrested, locked up and told to shut up about Jesus. However, rather than respond with fear to these threats, Peter and John responded with radical faith...

» *When you are fearful/intimidated/anxious—who/what do you turn to?*

» *After being released, where did Peter and John go and what did they do?*

» *What do you make of their prayer request (v 29-30)? What would you have prayed about?*

» *God came through spectacularly for Peter and John (v 31). Who could you pray with and how should you pray as you follow Jesus and face your fears?*

CHAPTER 7

LEAVE YOUR MARK

WALKING IN THE HALL OF HEROES
WARRIORS OF LEGACY

"WHAT WE DO IN LIFE
ECHOES IN ETERNITY"

MAXIMUS DECIMUS MERIDIUS

I n the centre of my hometown is a huge set of iron gates that lead into Pontypool park. For years I used to glance at the poppy wreaths honouring fallen British soldiers that adorn the gates as I travelled past them. Recently I stopped to take a closer look. It was a sobering moment.

Huge plaques dominate the gates bearing the names of the hundreds of men who laid down their lives in the name of freedom in the Great Wars of the 20th century. As I ran my finger over the cold metal print, it struck me that these men are real heroes. Men who died for king and country and whose courageous sacrifice should be celebrated, not forgotten. Yet for so long I was too busy and too self-absorbed to stop and to really take in what these men had done. Sadly, I think that is true of many of us.

As we come to our final chapter in this book, I want to urge you not to make the same mistake. After hanging out with various individual members of The Hard Corps—the poster boys, if you like—we now come to a long list of names, not dissimilar to the plaques at the park gates.

Some of these names are quite bizarre, and some are hard to pronounce, though a few might be familiar to you. This is the Hall of Heroes, the place where the full platoon of mighty men is remembered. Where every warrior is honoured. All that I ask is that you don't disregard this Roll of Honour with a drive-by glance, but rather that you humbly take time to read each name. That as you walk the corridors of the Hall of Heroes your footsteps would echo with respect.

OK, come with me...

Asahel the brother of Joab was one of the thirty;

 Elhanan the son of Dodo of Bethlehem,

Shammah of Harod,

 Elika of Harod,

Helez the Paltite,

 Ira the son of Ikkesh of Tekoa,

Abiezer of Anathoth,

 Mebunnai the Hushathite,

Zalmon the Ahohite,

 Maharai of Netophah,

Heleb the son of Baanah of Netophah,

 Ittai the son of Ribai of Gibeah of the people of Benjamin,

Benaiah of Pirathon,

 Hiddai of the brooks of Gaash,

Abi-albon the Arbathite,

 Azmaveth of Bahurim,

Eliahba the Shaalbonite, the sons of Jashen,

 Jonathan,

Shammah the Hararite,

 Ahiam the son of Sharar the Hararite,

Eliphelet the son of Ahasbai of Maacah,

 Eliam the son of Ahithophel of Gilo,

Hezro of Carmel,

 Paarai the Arbite,

Igal the son of Nathan of Zobah,

 Bani the Gadite,

Zelek the Ammonite,

 Naharai of Beeroth,

 the armor-bearer of Joab the son of Zeruiah,

Ira the Ithrite,

 Gareb the Ithrite,

Uriah the Hittite.

2 Samuel 23 v 24-39

Along with Abishai and Benaiah, who we have already met, here are the names of the rest of the Thirty. There are 37 warriors listed, which implies that some joined the number when others had fallen in battle. But these are mighty men of valour. Men who left their mark and whose names will forever be etched into the pages of Scripture. That we are still talking about them 3000 years later is a testimony to the legacy that they have left.

That's challenging.

Too often as men we live for the moment, often with little or no regard for the future effects of our daily lives. Do you ever stop and wonder what legacy you are going to leave? The truth is that every decision and every action will leave a legacy. The question: is what kind of legacy will it be? Bill Clinton rightly said: *"You know, it's just one small step from legacy to lame duck"*. I can only speak for myself here, but I don't want to be remembered as a lame duck! For what it's worth, I want my life to count. If you're with me, then let's see if we can glean some final inspiration from the ranks of the Hard Corps.

Family legacy

I love Christmas time for many reasons[1]. One of my favourites is that I get to see my kids perform in their school Christmas concerts.

The most memorable (to date) was when my daughter, Elen, sang *Away in a Manger* as a solo. She was only 4 at the time and I still remember it vividly. The hall fell silent and the eyes of all the kids, teachers and parents were fixed on her. As the spot light lit up her gorgeous angel costume, she clutched the microphone and just went for it. And boy did she nail it?! I can't lie—my hand was trembling as I was film-

---

1   Jesus, my family, vintage films and Terry's chocolate oranges, to name just a few...

ing it, tears streaming down my cheeks. I was just so proud of my baby! When she finished I could overhear other parents whispering to each other things like: *"Aw, bless her. That was amazin'!"* and *"She did so well."* I just wanted to stand up on my chair and shout at the top of my lungs:

"That's my little girl. She rocks!!"

I share that story because the families of the Hard Corps warriors would have felt exactly the same. You might have noticed that many of the names in the Roll of Honour are followed by the words *"the son of"*[2]. This might sound obvious, but the exemplary way in which these men fought for their king would have been a source of great honour for their families. You can just imagine proud parents hearing of the heroic military exploits of their son, or seeing him ride into town alongside the king, and wanting to tell everyone: *"That's my boy!"*

As men of God, surely we want to have the same effect on our own families. For our parents to glow when they hear our names mentioned. For our wives to speak of us with genuine affection and for our kids to proudly tell their friends: *"I want to be like my dad!"*

As a pastor I'm perhaps more aware than most of the danger of leaving a good legacy in my public ministry, yet failing miserably in my own home. My family are my first flock and as such I want to serve them well. I want to speak words that build up, encourage and breed security. I want to exemplify faith, hope and love; and when I screw up, I want to model humble repentance. I want the lasting legacy of my life to be

---

2 My favourite is "the sons of Jashen" (v 32) because it sounds like Sean Connery trying to say "the sons of Jason"!

a family that is fluent in the gospel, passionate about people, addicted to grace and buzzin' about the local church.

A family who know and love Jesus better because I was part of it. I want my wife and all my kids to be able to say of me: *"We learned to love Jesus by the way he loved us!"*

Rewrite history

I am very aware that I am part of my parents' legacy. There is no doubt that I am the product of their prayers, tears and many years of faithful gospel witness. However, not all of you reading this book had parents like mine.

Perhaps your parents don't know Jesus. Perhaps you're part of a family that has been damaged by divorce, shattered by bereavement or scarred by generations of alcoholism and abuse. Maybe you've bought the lie that because your family is screwed up, your life is destined to go to the dogs too. If that's you, you need to meet Eliam.

This man was a true and loyal soldier. We know this because his name is on the Roll of Honour. However, check out who his dad is—Ahithophel of Gilo. Now you might not be too familiar with this guy so let me give you some background.

Ahithophel worked for King David as his trusted counsellor, and he was incredibly good at his job.[3] However, the counsellor soon turned traitor and he joined Absalom in his conspiracy to overthrow the throne. Ahithophel's most heinous crimes include inciting Absalom to publicly rape his father's concubines and plotting to murder David in cold blood. When his plan failed, Ahithophel felt his only option was to commit suicide. He was found hanging at the family home.

Talk about messed up. Eliam's dad was a murderous traitor

---

3 "Now in those days the counsel that Ahithophel gave was as if one consulted the word of God; so was all the counsel of Ahithophel esteemed" (2 Samuel 16 v 23)

whose life and death were marked by shame. What if Eliam had believed the lie that his life was destined to go the same way as his dad's? How different his legacy would have been! But he didn't go the same way; he broke the cycle.

The gospel empowers you to do likewise:

> You were ransomed from the futile ways inherited from your forefathers, not with perishable things such as silver or gold, but with the precious blood of Christ".
>
> **1 Peter 1 v 18-19**

This has been the story of so many of my brothers and sisters at Hill City Church, who, by God's grace, have been able to completely rewrite their history. You can do the same. Through the finished work of Jesus, your legacy can be one of honour not dishonour. Grace, not disgrace. Life, not death.

That's epic!

Community legacy

William Shakespeare did it for Stratford upon Avon.

The Jacksons did it for Gary, Indiana.

Ali G did it for Staines.

In the same way, the men of The Hard Corps also put their towns on the map. Again, if you cast your eye over the list of warriors, you'll find out where many of them came from. I mean, had you ever heard of Tekoa, Pirathon or the brooks of Gaash before meeting this lot? Nor had I.

But for those who lived in each of the villages, towns and cities that these guys hailed from, these warriors were local heroes. Every battle fought and every act of courage in the name of the king served to bless the people of the communities from which they came.

As soldiers fighting for King Jesus, the challenge for us is: *what kind of legacy will we leave on our communities?*

Do we see our homes and our churches as places to hide in, or outposts from which to champion grace, hope and justice in Jesus' name? Are we active in our streets and schools, involved in sports teams, clubs and community action projects? Do we gripe about the gangs of youth who roam the streets or do we get our hands dirty and get to know them?

I planted the church I am pastor of several years ago, yet most of those outside the church don't know me as Pastor Dai; they still call me DJ Dai. That's because my first meaningful involvement in the community was teaching kids how to mix records together.

Is that gospel ministry? **Yes!**

Everything that we do in Jesus' name leaves a legacy. True warriors of the King will affect their communities. Their legacy will be souls saved, lives transformed, marriages healed, families reconciled, crime reduced and joy in the streets.

» I don't want streets named after me; I want the streets turned upside down by the gospel.

» I want my community to be a better place because a man of God lived there.

» I want my legacy to be one of gospel impact.

What about you?

Hitt where it hurts

There is one name that is etched in the Hall of Heroes that I have to confess gives me goose-bumps every time I read it.

You won't come to it until the very end of the list, having already encountered every other member of the Hard Corps. Here, right at the bottom is the name Uriah the Hittite. If the name rings a bell but you can't quite place him, let me help.

While Uriah was faithfully at war, King David was having sex with Uriah's wife, Bathsheba. When Bathsheba fell pregnant, David then arranged for Uriah to die in battle, in order to cover his tracks. It was the most shameful episode of David's life and the legacy of his lustful decision was devastating.

As we come to the end of our encounter with The Hard Corps, you have to wonder why the name that reminds everyone about the adultery, murder and shame of the king is put at the very end? Surely it would have been better to put a more inspiring name there—a name to arouse passion and stir up heroic courage, not kick us in the nuts!

For what it's worth, I believe that the decision to end on Uriah is for our encouragement.

Why?

Because it would be easy to read the stories of David and his mighty men and come away thinking *"I could never be like those guys. They were so strong, so brave and so godly. Me? I'm weak. I'm flawed. I'm guilty!"*

But God doesn't want you to step out of the Hall of Heroes feeling like that. By signing off with Uriah the Hittite, the Holy Spirit is reminding us that King David, the man after God's own heart, was in fact a vile sinner in as much need of grace as we are. As heartening as it is to look at The Hard Corps and their beloved king, it's crucial that we lift our eyes higher. We need to look to David's King, Jesus, the sinless Saviour who forgives sin, gives epic grace and makes gospel warriors out of guilty wretches.

He is truly a King worth fighting for.

Eternal legacy

Perhaps the most striking thing about the Hard Corps is that their legacy wasn't short-term; it was eternal. By aligning themselves with King David, they were serving the kingdom of God, and with every victory won they were fulfilling His eternal purposes on earth.

That's phenomenal.

But wait, we're part of the same story too, right? We also get to fight for the King and leave an eternal legacy because Jesus Himself has hand-picked us, redeemed us and given us a part to play in His salvation master plan! Wow!! If we really grasped that, then surely our lives would look radically different. As Billy Graham put so well:

"Our days are numbered. One of the primary goals in our lives should be to prepare for our last day. The legacy we leave is not just in our possessions, but in the quality of our lives. What preparations should we be making now? The greatest waste in all of our earth, which cannot be recycled or reclaimed, is our waste of the time that God has given us each day."

Soldier of Christ, one day you're going to die and you will stand before the King.

Do you really want your legacy to be how many girls you slept with, how much money you made or how much beer you could drink?

Do you want to be remembered as a man who risked nothing and achieved nothing?

Do you really want your obituary to read: *"I got 5,000,000 points while escaping from demon monkeys in Temple Run. Beat that!"*?[4]

That's not a legacy.

That's a tragedy.

---

4   Temple Run is a popular and insanely addictive game that is played on smart phones and tablets. Many hours of life can be wasted running away from imaginary, pixellated demon monkeys. *Exactly...*

Surely as men of God the legacy that we should be striving to leave is the legacy of a life poured out in the service of the King. A life of holding out the Word of life to the dying, imploring them to turn to Jesus and trust His gospel to save them. There is simply no greater cause!

I'll never forget the time I was asked to preach at a men's meeting at a small Welsh chapel near Swansea. I turned up and sat at the back of the hall and could tell that my presence was making many of the men (who didn't know that I was the speaker) feel uneasy. They were giving me those *"he must be out on day release"* eyes.

I get that a lot.

As I got up to speak, there was definitely a nervous tension in the room. Uneasy eyes quickly widened into *"Oh my days, he's the preacher!"* eyes! I was well into my rant when I noticed an elderly gentlemen sitting in the front row. He was animated, alive and loving the word of God. He didn't recognise me, but I certainly recognised him.

After the service, still not recognising me, he came and told me: *"I'm so sorry. When you came in, I thought that you were an unbeliever and I spent the first half of the meeting praying that God would save you!"*

I was able to tell him that God had already answered his prayer many years earlier. This wonderful old man was Owen Jones, the chaplain of the youth camp I had attended back in 1992. It was the gospel that he preached that week that finally conquered my heart!

He was totally blown away!

It's not every day you get to catch a glimpse of the legacy that you will leave behind. But that's exactly what I am—a small part of Owen Jones' eternal legacy. A soul snatched from hell through his faithful ministry.

It was such a precious moment and one that will live with me for ever. However, it was also a moment that got me thinking—we haven't got a clue what God is going to do in the lives of those we're touching with the gospel. The next Spurgeon might be in your Sunday School class, workplace or even your house right now.

That's a phenomenal thought!

So whether at home, at work, in church or in your community, let's be all about leaving an eternal legacy of lives transformed by the grace and for the glory of Jesus. I don't know about you, but when all is said and done, I want my life to have mattered. I want to leave my mark. I want to stand before my King battle-weary but surrounded by men, women and children whose souls I went to war for. I might be sporting a thousand scars but every one will tell a story of gospel conquest. I want to be able to say with Paul:

> I have fought the good fight, I have finished the race, I have kept the faith.
>
> **2 Timothy 4 v 7**

The legacy that we leave will ultimately be decided by the decisions we make today. We only get one shot at this life so let's not waste it by laying up treasures on earth. Let's get going, live for the glory of our King and take as many with us as we can.

Let's be men who leave an eternal legacy.

> Therefore, since we are surrounded by so great a cloud of witnesses, let us also lay aside every weight, and sin which clings so closely, and let us run with endurance the race that is set before us, looking to Jesus, the founder and perfecter of our faith, who for the joy that was set before him endured the cross, despising the shame, and is seated at the right hand of the throne of God.
>
> **Hebrews 12 v 1-3**

COMBAT TRAINING

Session 7
Growing as a warrior of legacy

Walking through the corridors of the Hall of David's heroes is a sobering experience. These great men of honour lived lives of epic significance and, as such, their names and legacy live on. Incredibly, that's exactly what God wants for all of us. Jesus' salvation work on earth has been fulfilled, but that's far from the end of the story. His mission continues, His legacy remains— and we are part of it...

Read Luke 24 v 36-49

» *As Jesus prepared to return to heaven, He gathered His boys together and told them that it was now their time to shine. What did He entrust them with? (v44-48)*

» *How do you think the disciples would have responded to this commission?*

» *The gospel baton has been handed down to every generation of believers ever since. Where are you at with it?*

» *What help/encouragement did Jesus give to His disciples as He prepared to depart?*

» *What help do you need from Jesus to effectively play your part in this great gospel story?*

While there is no question that Jesus is the über-hero of Scripture, it's still helpful to consider other warriors of faith, like the Hard Corps, whose faith, courage and passion for God can encourage us as we seek to fight the good fight and live life like it matters. If you're not sure where to find such men, God has kindly blessed us with a Faith Hero telephone directory...

Read Hebrews 11 v 1 – 12 v 2

» *Which of these heroes of the faith most inspire you? Why?*

» *What other gospel warriors (alive or dead) have most impacted your life? In what way(s)?*

» *What kind of legacy do you want to leave and to whom?*

» *What do you need to do (lifestyle, focus, priorities, repentance etc.) to ensure that you leave a positive, gospel legacy that blesses others and glorifies your King?*

Do it!

OUTRO

As we conclude our time in the trenches with the Hard Corps, it would be worth our while reflecting on all that we've learned from these mighty warriors.

Hopefully *JB's* courageous faith has inspired us to defy the odds and live strong as men of faith in a hostile culture.

The iron fist and swashbuckling skills of *Eleazar* certainly gave us fresh incentive to tighten our grip on God's word, and *Shammah's* epic bean-field stand-off surely makes us want to fight with all we've got to protect what God has entrusted to us.

The exploits of the *Three Nameless Ninjas* can't fail to ignite passion in our hearts for King Jesus, and I would expect that we all took a kicking in the pride department when confronted by the humility of *Abishai.*

And there's no way that the insanely courageous antics of *Benaiah* haven't filled us with fresh resolve to man up and lay the smack down on our fears.

Finally, as we walked the hallowed corridors of the *Hall of Heroes,* didn't your heart beat a little faster as you contemplated what it was going to take to be a man who leaves a lasting legacy for the glory of God?

However, if it's the warriors of the Hard Corps who have left the greatest impression on us, then we have spectacularly missed the point of what their incredible lives were all about; and I have failed dismally as an author!

The point is that, regardless of how impressive an art exhibition on display in a gallery may be, *it's the artist and not the individual pieces of art* who gets the credit. In the same way, the feats of courageous passion and devastating military skill exemplified by the Hard Corps were really the work of one much greater—*Jesus Christ.* Therefore, while we should rightly applaud the heroics of David's Mighty Men, surely the most appropriate response is to go a step further and fully surrender our lives to the same God who they fought for.

That's a crazy thought, isn't it?

That we can actually step up and fight in the ranks of the same army of the same great King as the Thirty and the Three. That before God, the soldiers of the Hard Corps are in no way greater than any of us. Rather, they're our brothers in the gospel, who we stand in line with, shoulder to shoulder.

On the surface they might have looked more impressive than many of us, but in reality they were just as dependent on His grace as we are. They knew who they were fighting for and they knew who fought for them. And that same God is as faithful to His people today as He was back then. I hope that excites you. I pray that gives you courage!

Let's be men who wage war in the true Spirit of the Hard Corps.

Let's be men of fearless faith, ferocious passion and reckless gospel abandon.

Let's be men who live for a cause that is infinitely greater than ourselves.

Let's be men who leave behind us a legacy of grace-changed lives.

And may Christ the King get all the glory for it.

THE ARMOURY

Warriors need weapons, and regular training in how to use them. Listed below are some of the many books, courses, websites and other resources available to help us contend for the gospel.

Books

Cross Centred Life; Humility
CJ Mahaney

Captured by a Better Vision; You Can Change
Tim Chester:

The Code Carl Beech

Rescuing Ambition
Dave Harvey

Don't Waste Your Life; Desiring God John Piper

Crazy Love Francis Chan

Disciplines of a Godly Man; Disciplines of a Godly Family
Kent Hughes

The Meaning of Marriage; Generous Justice; Counterfeit Gods Tim Keller

The Barbarian Way
Erwin MacManus

Sex is not the Problem (Lust is) Joshua Harris

The Explicit Gospel
Matt Chandler

Leaders Who Last Dave Kraft

Recovering Biblical Manhood & Womanhood
John Piper and Wayne Grudem

Jesus + Nothing = Everything Tullian Tchividjian

Bible Overview Steve Levy

Gospel-Centred Discipleship
Kevin Dodson

Death By Love Mark Driscoll

Holiness JC Ryle

The Enemy Within
Kris Lundgaard

Scandalous D A Carson

The Manual Bible notes for men from CVM

A Few Good Men
Richard Coekin

Men of God Trevor Archer & Tim Thornborough

Fatherhood Tony Payne

Every Man's Battle
S Arterburn & F Stoeker

The Big Fight Richard Perkins & Tim Thornborough

Bible studies and courses

Gospel-Centred Life
Gospel-Centred Church
Gospel-Centred Marriage
Gospel-Centred Family
Gospel-Centred Leadership
Man of God
Discipleship Explored
One2One: Real men
The World We All Want
The Manual (CVM)

Websites/software

Covenant Eyes
Accountability and filtering software
www.covenanteyes.com

Safe Eyes
Protects your family from harmful online content
www.internetsafety.com/
safeeyes

Christianity Explored
Evangelistic website with great testimonies.
www.christianityexplored.org

The Gospel Coalition
Great site for book reviews, blogs and insight
www.gospelcoalition.org

Explore App
Daily Bible readings direct to your smart phone / tablet
www.thegoodbook.co.uk

Ministries
Shift
Seeking to bring about a culture shift in Jesus' name
www.shift-uk.com

Desiring God
Resources from John Piper
www.desiringgod.org

The Good Book Company
Bible centred resources
www.thegoodbook.co.uk

CVM - Christian Vision for Men: www.cvm.org.uk

Christian Conventions
Organises Bible-teaching conventions for men in the UK.
www.christianconventions.org.uk

True Freedom Trust
Help for those those struggling with same sex attraction
www.truefreedomtrust.co.uk

ACKNOWLEDGEMENTS

It took almost four years from my first encounter with David's mighty warriors in the pages of Scripture to the publication of the book in your hands. It really has been an incredible journey and one that would not have been possible were it not for the gracious help of some great people. This section is about honouring and acknowledging them.

Firstly, a huge thank you to the guys at the Good Book Company for believing in this project and giving a chopsy, grammatically-challenged gospel ranter from Wales the opportunity to put his passion for The Hard Corps down in print. I'm also deeply grateful for the patience and understanding you showed during my 18 month "break" while I focused on serving my family following the birth of our twins.

Secondly, massive gratitude has to go to Tim Thornborough—a fantastic editor who has become a firm friend and whose insight, humour and passion for the gospel has significantly impacted and inspired my writing. The best parts of this book came about thanks to your input. Mercifully, the worst parts of this book never made it to print thanks to your discernment. Thanks fella!

Nuff respect has to go to my co-pastor / co-pilot / co-warrior, James Richards, one of my best mates and a true gospel ninja. Bruv,

I couldn't have taken the time I needed to smash this book out if you hadn't been both willing and able to hold the fort at Hill City, so thanks for giving me the space and the grace to get this done.

As far as the writing process goes, big up Starbucks for free wifi and free refills. Big up my dad for letting me spend hours upon end parked in front of his log fire to write during the winter months. Big love also to Jeff and Jen Taylor for wonderful friendship, warm hospitality and the provision of a writing "den" when I needed it.

To my best friend and beautiful wife, Michelle, thanks so much for your love, support, encouragement and *cwtches*[1] throughout this whole process. Your passion for Christ, your love for our kids, your heart for the lost and your zeal for the church continue to blow me away. I'm a better disciple and a better man because of you and there's no one I'd rather have by my side on this epic gospel adventure. Thank you so much babes! Also gotta give a shout out to the Hankey kids, Elen, Josiah, Ezra and Anastasia—you guys are all bonkers and you rock my world. I love being your dad. Thanks for blessing me with perspective and constantly reminding me of the amazing grace of God.

Finally, to Jesus, my Saviour and my King, thanks is far too small a word with which to convey how grateful I am to you for not only saving me, but also for giving me a cause, a ministry and a message to live and die for. I am nothing without your grace. I pray that the legacy of this book will be men transformed, families blessed and the gospel unleashed for your glory.

---

1   *Cwtch* (pronounced "cutch") is Welsh for a cuddle, but *cwtches* are way better than cuddles! Just saying...

Other titles for men

A Few Good Men
by Richard Coekin

A Few Good Men presents the reader with 10 positive role models from the Bible. From obedient Noah to loyal Onesiphorous, these character sketches combine dramatic story-telling with challenging and insightful comment. Solidly founded on biblical narrative, these chapters will challenge and inspire readers to examine the struggles and temptations of these biblical men who faced the same struggles that men still face today.

Men of God

Has there ever been a more urgent time for Christian men to stand up and be counted? This book is designed to encourage Christian men to live for Christ: in their homes; in their workplaces; in their leisure; and in their churches.

Contributions from John Benton, Richard Coekin, Phillip Jensen, David Jackman, Hugh Palmer, Vaughan Roberts, William Taylor, Rico Tice, John Tindall, Trevor Archer and Tim Thornborough.

Rock Solid: Men of Truth

Rock Solid aims to help us get to grips with Christian truth. If faith is not lived out, it is worth nothing. This book explains and clarifies twelve important and powerful doctrines, or "themes", from the Bible, so that we might have the comfort and assurance that comes from them, and so that we can make our life decisions by them. Ideal for groups to read so that they can get a clear hold on the truths that define who we are as followers of Christ.

Edited by Tim Thornborough & Trevor Archer

Bible studies for men

Man of God *10 studies*
by Sam Allberry and Anthony Bewes

This set of Bible studies aims to unpack the answers the Bible gives to the question of identity that men face today. We will learn our God-given role in creation, and how that has been ruined by the fall. And we will discover how we can start to be restored through the man above all men—Jesus Christ. Some things will be controversial in our culture. This course doesn't set out to be politically correct but faithful to God's counter-cultural word.

David: God's true king *6 studies*
by Nathan Buttery

We love David the hero, the shepherd boy who became king of Israel, chosen by God as a man "after His own heart". This Good Book Guide on the life of David reveals the secret of David's success and the reasons for his many failures. But it also uncovers the greater story of a better hero. You will learn how this weak king points us to the ultimate King—despised, rejected, yet finally winning the ultimate victory for His people over sin and death.

One2One: Real Men *by Carl Laferton*

- What does it mean to be a real man?
- What difference will being a Christian make to my life?

This one2one Bible-study guide is designed to help a teenage guy and an older man explore together what it means to grow into genuine Christian maturity. Through the 14 sessions in this step-by-step guide—seven done together, and seven on your own—you'll discover from the book of Ephesians how to live as you were designed to.

BIBLICAL | RELEVANT | ACCESSIBLE

At The Good Book Company, we are dedicated to helping Christians and local churches grow. We believe that God's growth process always starts with hearing clearly what he has said to us through his timeless word—the Bible.

Ever since we opened our doors in 1991, we have been striving to produce Bible-based resources that bring glory to God. We have grown to become an international provider of user-friendly resources to the Christian community, with believers of all backgrounds and denominations using our books, Bible studies, devotionals, evangelistic resources, and DVD-based courses.

We want to equip ordinary Christians to live for Christ day by day, and churches to grow in their knowledge of God, their love for one another, and the effectiveness of their outreach.

Call us for a discussion of your needs or visit one of our local websites for more information on the resources and services we provide.

Your friends at The Good Book Company

thegoodbook.com | thegoodbook.co.uk
thegoodbook.com.au | thegoodbook.co.nz
thegoodbook.co.in